SPIDERS
AND OTHER ARACHNIDS

Modern Biology

General Editor
J. E. Webb, Ph.D., D.Sc.
Professor of Zoology
Westfield College, University of London

SPIDERS
AND OTHER
ARACHNIDS

THEODORE SAVORY, M.A., F.Z.S.

 THE ENGLISH UNIVERSITIES PRESS LTD
102 NEWGATE STREET · LONDON · EC1

First printed 1964

Printed in Great Britain for the English Universities Press Ltd
by T. & A. Constable Ltd, Hopetoun Street, Edinburgh

Editor's Foreword

The Series

THE Modern Biology series, in which this book is included, is intended to provide the background knowledge to botany and zoology that the sixth forms in schools and students in their early years at university need but are unlikely to find in the general textbooks. Each book will give a short authoritative account of an important aspect, a general topic or a new development in biology clearly presented in an extended essay form by an established teacher or research worker in his own field of study.

Scientific matter usually makes heavy demands on the powers of concentration of the reader. Complicated facts and theories are inherently difficult to express in everyday language and frequently hard to understand. Nevertheless much can be done to ease the burden, not only through clear exposition both in text and illustration, but also in the layout and typography of a book. As editor, I have done what I can in planning the form of this book to ensure that there is no block to understanding arising from sheer physical difficulty of reading. For instance, the type face and the length and spacing of the lines is such that the book can be read with ease by any normally sighted person.

This is, perhaps, an experiment in popularization, but not through the over-simplification of ideas and the avoidance of technicalities which inevitably lead to loss of accuracy. The books in this series are intended to be read as one would read a novel—from cover to cover. There is something in them for all who care to do so. For the student it is hoped they will at once provide examples of the art of the essay in science and a new outlook on biology which will encourage wider reading.

This Book

Spiders and their allies, the scorpions, have interested Man since earliest times. However, they are only two of a number of related forms which zoologists include in the class Arachnida. Arachnids have a long fossil history extending far back into geological time and rival the insects in their diversity of form and habits. Nevertheless, as a group for study, they tend to have been neglected. Why this should be so is not easy to understand. Perhaps it is due to the abhorrence some people feel for them, or it may follow from the venomous nature of certain of the larger species. On the other hand, it may be that insufficient attention has been paid to their systematics so that they are often difficult to identify. Whatever is the cause it is certainly true that arachnids are far less well known than the insects. This is a pity for, as Mr. Theodore Savory shows in his new book *Spiders and other Arachnids*, these animals are admirable subjects for the demonstration of the interrelation of structure, function and behaviour, both in the classroom and in the field.

His account is centred about the spider and its biology. Enough anatomy is briefly given for an appreciation of the relevance of web-spinning, courtship, mating and other aspects of behaviour in the lives of these unusual but highly successful animals. Much of this behaviour can be watched with very little difficulty in common spiders from the house or garden kept in simple vivaria. However, Mr. Savory has not neglected the lesser known arachnids both large and small, some of which are bizarre, many of medical and economic importance and all of intrinsic interest. Among these less familiar forms, too, are some, such as the false scorpions and harvestmen, that can readily be collected and kept alive in the laboratory for observation and experiment. They make a rewarding study for the student.

Mr. Savory, in writing, has had the needs of the upper forms in schools in mind, but there is also much here both for the university student and for the general reader. He leaves one with an abiding interest in the group and a desire to look for and watch the habits of these animals in the home and the countryside.

J. E. WEBB

Preface

I HAVE written this short account of spiders, their phenomena and their problems, having in mind the needs of serious students of zoology, who may be either above the average A-level candidates or may be first-year university undergraduates. This implies that I have assumed my readers to have as much knowledge of Arthropoda as follows familiarity with the crayfish and the cockroach; it also implies that comparable knowledge of the spider is desirable and should be as accurately known. No attempt is made to burden the student with the specialized aspects of arachnology, but rather to provide a base from which any zoologist who contemplates specialization in an undeniably interesting group of animals should be able to make an intelligent and well-founded start. A full-scale treatise to help him on his way is at present in active preparation.

T. H. S.

Acknowledgments

MY thanks are due to Professor J. E. Webb for his helpfully constructive criticism, to Miss E. Allsopp for Figures 29-32, to Mr. Barry Goater for Figures 38 and 39 and 42-50; also for permission to reproduce illustrations from my earlier books to Messrs. Arnolds for Figures 5, 7, 8, 10 and 16; Messrs. Sidgwick & Jackson for Figures 15 and 19, Messrs. Frederick Warne for Figures 1, 2 and 23; and the Pergamon Press for Figure 52.

Contents

Contents

List of Illustrations

List of Illustrations

1 *About Arachnids*

IT is appropriate, in an introduction to a study of spiders, to begin with a reference to the great antiquity of the class, Arachnida, to which they, with scorpions, harvestmen and mites, belong, and of which they make up the greater part. Nearly all the fossils from the Silurian rocks, and all those from older strata, are the remains of the many creatures that lived in the primaeval seas and rivers of the Palaeozoic era. This may perhaps have been five hundred million years ago; and among the animals of that far-distant period there have been found a number of specimens of scorpions that differ only in unimportant details from the scorpions that live today. In consequence zoologists accept the conclusion that scorpions were among the first of all animals to leave the water, abandon an aquatic life, and begin the colonization and occupation of the land.

No fossil spiders of the same, Silurian, epoch have yet been found, but this cannot be taken as proof that they or their immediate ancestors are not waiting for some fortunate geologist to come upon them in the future. Thus we have no certain knowledge what the forerunners of spiders were like, but from the Carboniferous rocks, perhaps a hundred million years later, fossil remains of spiders and of nearly all the other orders of the class Arachnida have been recovered in reasonable numbers. It is of interest to note that only the earliest insects were in existence at this time, while the "flies", on which most spiders largely depend today, did not appear until the Jurassic period, about another hundred million years later.

The whole story of the evolution of spiders is thus a very difficult one to tell with certainty; it can be told only with the help of speculation and imagination, so that it is no surprise that different writers have often expressed different opinions. They have suggested, for example, that webs arose from silk used to cover the eggs, or from the "drag-line" that spiders trail behind them. This makes it unprofitable to pursue the matter any further at this stage: but the great antiquity of spiders, prominent as they were among the earliest inhabitants of the world, is beyond question.

Man, therefore, must have found scorpions and spiders all round him from the first, and some of the oldest civilizations have left records which show us how they were impressed by the obvious peculiarities of these undeniably remarkable little animals. Scorpions were the more conspicuous, and when, about four thousand years ago, the apparent path of the sun in the sky was divided into the twelve parts of the zodiac, the scorpion was taken as the sign of the eighth part. The crab was the only other invertebrate to be thus distinguished.

The Persians looked upon the scorpion as one of the agents of evil, and often portrayed it in opposition to their god Mithras; while the Egyptians associated it with Isis.

The spider is better known in Latin poetry, for Ovid has told the story of its origin in the *Metamorphoses*. Arachne was a maiden of Lydia, renowned for her skill as a seamstress, and foolhardy enough to challenge Pallas Athene to a contest in weaving. She was victorious; but Pallas, enraged by defeat, transformed her into a spider and condemned her to spin for ever.

Zoologists today put scorpions and spiders into two orders, Scorpiones and Araneae or Araneida, of the class Arachnida, one of the classes of the great phylum Arthropoda. This phylum, which includes more than half a million species, is of importance both in the academic world of the laboratory and in the economic sphere. There is no need to emphasize the importance of the Insecta, which form its largest class; for insects are valuable scavengers, helpful in the pollination of flowers and thus assisting in the production of fruits, and appreciated as food by many larger animals, such as birds and fishes, that are needed by man. At the same time insects attack our bodies and those of domesticated animals, they spread diseases of many kinds among herds and cultivated crops, and they attack stored materials whenever they find the opportunity to do so. They cannot be said to be adequately studied by the acquisition of a little knowledge of the cockroach, the honey-bee and the mosquito.

In the sea the part played on land by the Insecta is taken by the Crustacea. Some of these have a slight direct economic value, like the crabs and lobsters; the rest take their places in large numbers of food-chains, and are essential in the nourishment of the larger fish and the whales, which are equally essential to man. Again, a study of the crayfish provides but a fragmentary knowledge of the class as a whole.

The class Arachnida is, in general, almost wholly neglected; yet it should be clear from what has been said above that a balanced knowledge of zoology is not to be gained without considerable emphasis on the arthropods; and that adequate appreciation of this phylum can only follow a broadening of the horizon so as to include the class of arachnids.

There can be no surprise that among the many species that go to make up the phylum Arthropoda there are very great differences in size, in structure, in habitats and in behaviour. This large multitude seems to divide itself into four main groups, or sub-phyla, and their separation from each other must have taken place at a very early stage in the evolution of the phylum.

There are two small sub-phyla, the Onycophora, which include the important and curious creatures with apparent resemblances to the annelids, and known as Peripatus; and the Pantopoda, a group of purely marine animals called sea-spiders or Pycnogonida. These two lines of descent we must neglect.

The two larger sub-phyla are the Mandibulata, sometimes called the Antennata, and the Chelicerata, two groups which are obviously characterized and distinguished by the possession on the one hand of antennae and mandibles, and on the other hand by the possession of chelicerae.

The Mandibulata include the Crustacea, Myriapoda and Insecta.

Among the Chelicerata there are both aquatic and terrestrial forms. The king-crab, Limulus, and its extinct allies, the Eurypterida, form the class Merostomata; the majority of the Chelicerata are land-dwellers and form the class Arachnida, with which this book is concerned.

In the class Arachnida there are eleven living and five extinct orders. The latter will be neglected. The living orders are very different both in numbers and distribution; it is fair to say that six of them are of some general importance, while the others are the concern of specialists only. The names of the six are:

Araneida	spiders
Scorpiones	scorpions
Pseudoscorpiones	false-scorpions
Opiliones	harvestmen
Solifugae	wind-scorpions
Acari	mites and ticks

The spiders are by far the largest of these orders. The most reliable estimate puts the number of known species at about forty thousand, five or six times as many as the species of mites, the next largest order. The other orders contain between eight and twelve hundred species each, as far as is known at present.

The order of spiders will be treated in some detail in this book; the five other orders mentioned above will be more shortly described with sufficient detail to give a balanced picture of the class Arachnida.

2 *External Characteristics*

DIVISION of the body into segments, or somites, is a general feature of the Arthropoda, but almost all outward traces of this condition have disappeared from the body of a spider, and the most important of its external characteristics is its division into two parts only. These are loosely called the cephalothorax and the abdomen, but the terms prosoma and opisthosoma are to be preferred in exact writing, because the cephalothorax of a crustacean is not the same, either in the number of somites or the number and nature of its appendages, as the prosoma of an arachnid.

A spider's prosoma is covered by an unsegmented carapace, on which a groove often marks a boundary between what may be called the head region and the thorax. The true, morphological, head of a spider consists, however, of only one somite, and is therefore very different from the head of a crustacean or the separated head of an insect. A central dent or fovea in the carapace usually indicates the place to which the muscles of the stomach are attached within, and radiating depressions may similarly be formed by the muscles of the legs (Fig. 1). The lower surface of the prosoma is formed by a large sternum, surrounded by the basal joints of the appendages. The sternum is usually oval or heart-shaped, and like the carapace it shows no indication of segments. In front of it, in the middle line, lies the lower lip or labium. This is not to be confused with the labium of an insect, with which it is not homologous. It is probably the sternite of the second somite.

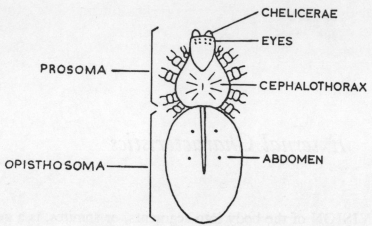

Figure 1. A spider: dorsal surface.

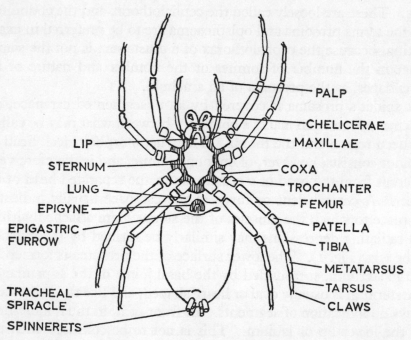

Figure 2. A spider: ventral surface.

The opisthosoma is similarly without evidence of its original segmentation, except in a few species belonging to a primitive East Asian sub-order.* It is joined to the prosoma by a narrow waist or pedicel, one of the structural features of the order. Its upper surface is sometimes spiny, but most often it is smooth, with a pattern in sombre colours. There is frequently a central mark, indicating the position of the heart beneath.

The lower surface of the opisthosoma carries the genital orifice just behind the pedicel, with the lung-books on each side, and an epigastric furrow, in which the respiratory spiracles lie, just behind. At the tip of the abdomen are the spinnerets, usually four or six in number (Fig. 2).

Critical examination, supported by evidence from the embryonic development of the animal, shows that in the body of an adult spider eighteen segments or somites are represented. There are six in the prosoma, as is evident from the six pairs of appendages which it carries. The seventh somite is the narrow pedicel, joining the two halves of the body and giving a relative mobility between them. In some spiders it is strengthened by minute chitinous plates above and below. The eighth somite is marked by the opening of the genital duct from the reproductive organs. This orifice is inconspicuous in the male; in the female it occupies the centre of an elaborate epigyne, different in every different species. The position of the genital orifice on the second somite of the opisthosoma is a characteristic feature of all arachnids. The eighth somite carries the first pair of lung-books, and where, as in some families, there are two pairs of these organs, the second pair is on the ninth somite. Alternatively, the ninth somite carries the respiratory spiracles, leading to tracheal tubes among the internal tissues. A great increase in the length of the tenth somite carries the spinnerets to their position at the tip of the abdomen. In the most primitive spiders there are four spinnerets belonging to the tenth and four to the eleventh somite, and they are placed near the middle of the opisthosoma. The remaining somites are all reduced to a small anal tubercle, not always easy to discern, a vestigial ending to the body.

* The classification of spiders is described later.

In addition to the metameric segments, the body of an arthropod may possess an acron in front and a telson behind. The acron, which may be compared to the prostomium of the earthworm, differs from the segments behind it both in development and in the fact that it never carries appendages. In spiders it is inconspicuous, being perhaps represented by the space in front of the eyes and above the chelicerae; but in some other orders it is not so inconspicuous. The telson is a tail-like addition to the last somite, and in some arachnids it is a long and active flagellum, but it is not present in spiders.

In all Arachnida there are six pairs of prosomatic appendages, namely the chelicerae, the pedipalpi and the four pairs of legs.

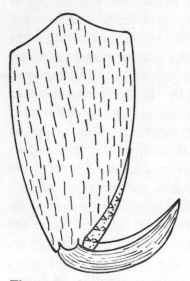

The chelicerae (Fig. 3), which are the only pair situated in front of the mouth, are the spider's weapons for attack and defence. They are in two parts, a broad basal one and a curved, sharply-pointed fang jointed to it.

In the large sub-order Araneomorphae to which most spiders belong the chelicerae move sideways, the fangs strike inwards and meet, or tend to meet, in the body of the prey. In the sub-order Mygalomorphae to which the trap-door spiders belong the chelicerae strike downwards and their fangs pierce the victim in parallel directions.

Figure 3. A spider's chelicera. All spiders are venomous. Within the first segment of each chelicera, or sometimes at each side of the forepart of the prosoma, there is a poison-secreting gland from which a duct leads to an orifice just inside the tip of the fang. The poison is quickly fatal to insects and to most arthropods, and there are plenty of well-authenticated records of its killing small vertebrates such as mice, birds and fish. Very few spiders are dangerous to man, and human beings are only rarely bitten, accidentally, by a spider which they have startled. There is usually no more than a temporary, trifling, irritation.

The notorious tarantula is an ordinary wolf-spider living in Italy and Spain. Its bite is no different from that of hundreds of other spiders, and cannot be the cause of "tarantism", a remarkable and largely imaginary complaint which was prevalent in these countries from the fifteenth to the eighteenth centuries. Contemporary accounts describe the effects of the spider's bite as including pain and swelling, paralysis, vomiting and melancholy, ending in death. The only cure was music, which induced frenzied dancing: the whole phenomenon of tarantism is slightly mysterious.

On the other hand, the poison of the "Black Widow", a name given to a number of species of the genus Latrodectus found in many parts of the world, can produce very serious effects in man, and sometimes death is the result. There are a few other species that are really dangerous, but there is no obvious reason why they are so different from the majority. The venom is an alkaline fluid containing proteins, and two varieties have been recognized. In some spiders it has a toxic effect on nervous tissue, in others a gangrenous action, destroying cells in general; and in some spiders the two types are mixed.

The chelicerae, the only appendages in front of the mouth, may be contrasted with the two pairs of antennae in front of the mouth of the crayfish. The appendages of the anterior segments of members of the three great classes of arthropods are compared in the following table:

Somite	CRAYFISH Head	SPIDER Prosoma	COCKROACH Head
1	None	Chelicerae	None
2	Antennules	Pedipalpi	Antennae
3	Antennae	Legs i	None
4	Mandibles	Legs ii	Mandibles
5	Maxillulae	Legs iii	Maxillae
6	Maxillae	Legs iv	Labium

Somite	CRAYFISH	SPIDER	COCKROACH
	Thorax	*Opisthosoma*	*Thorax*
7	Maxillipeds i	None (Pedicel)	Legs i
8	Maxillipeds ii	Lungs i	Legs ii
9	Maxillipeds iii	Lungs ii	Legs iii
			Abdomen
10	Cheliped	Spinnerets i	None
11	Legs i	Spinnerets ii	None
12	Legs ii	None	None
13	Legs iii	None	None
14	Legs iv	None	None
	Abdomen		
15	Pleopods i	None	None
16	Pleopods ii	None	None
17	Pleopods iii	None	None
18	Pleopods iv	None	None
19	Pleopods v	None	None
20	Uropods		Cerci

The value of this comparison lies in its demonstration of the different composition of the part sometimes called the cephalo-thorax. In the Crustacea a head of six somites and a thorax of eight together correspond to the first six somites in the Arachnida.

The appendages of the second pair, on the second adult somite, are known as the palpi or the pedipalpi. In the scorpions these are the great "claws"; in all spiders they are leg-like and are composed of six segments, coxa, trochanter, femur, patella, tibia, tarsus (Fig. 4). In all except mature male spiders the pedipalpi are sensory organs, clad with spines and setae of different lengths and diameters and probably all tactile in their function. The pedipalpi also possess organs of chemo-reception, to be described later.

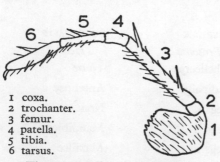

1 coxa.
2 trochanter.
3 femur.
4 patella.
5 tibia.
6 tarsus.

Figure 4. Female pedipalp.

The first (proximal or basal) segment of a pedipalp shows a feature that is characteristic of many of the Arachnida. This is the existence of an inwardly-directed lobe or gnathobase, often referred to as the maxilla, though not homologous with the maxillae of either insects or crustaceans, and used in crushing and squeezing the fluid contents out of the prey (Fig. 5). It is often furnished with "teeth", large or small, and it contains glands, known simply as the maxillary glands, the secretion of which starts the digestion of the spider's food.

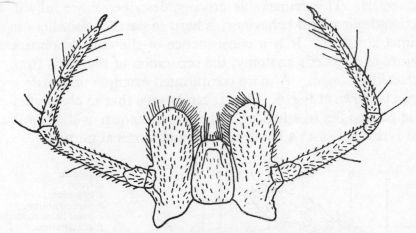

Figure 5. Lip, maxillae and pedipalpi of female spider.

The great interest of the pedipalpi of spiders lies in their remarkable modification among males, for whom they act as accessory sex organs.

The last or tarsal segment of the palp usually ends in a claw both among females and young males, and the segment itself is of the normal cylindrical form. An immature male spider cannot therefore be distinguished as such. When it has cast its skin for the last time but one, the tarsal segment can be seen to be enlarged, looking more like a thumb than a finger. When the last moult takes place, the whole segment has changed.

There is no claw and the segment itself has assumed a spoon-like form: in the bowl of the spoon lies the male organ. These organs vary a great deal. Some are simple, some are remarkably complex, and in no two species are they alike. Hence a close inspection of the organ is the most certain way of determining the identity of a male, a fact which gives male spiders an enhanced value in the eyes of collectors, who understandably regret their comparative scarcity. At all times of the year females are far more numerous.

The most primitive form of these organs is that of a simple syringe, the function of which is to take up a drop of seminal fluid from the special "sperm-web", which the male spider has made for its reception, to store it, and subsequently to transfer it to the body of the female. This remarkable process, described more fully in the section dealing with behaviour, is hard to parallel elsewhere in the animal kingdom. It is a consequence of the equally remarkable feature of a spider's anatomy, the separation of the testis from the intromittent organ. A more complicated example of a male tarsal organ is shown at Fig. 6. Here it can be seen that an elaborate piece of apparatus lies in a hollow of the tarsus, known as the cymbium, and is divisible into a basal, median and terminal portions.

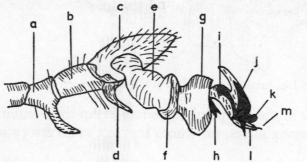

a patella.
b tibia.
c cymbium.
d paracymbium.
e basal haematodocha.
f subtegulum.
g tegulum.
h median apophysis.
i radix
j lateral subterminal apophysis.
k terminal apophysis.
l conductor.
m embolus.

Figure 6. Palpal organ of a male Linyphiid spider.

The first of these is a soft expansible sac known as the haematodocha, which during mating is distended with blood and produces the pressure necessary for the ejaculation of the sperm. The middle part, covered by the tegulum, contains the reservoir of the receptaculum seminis. The terminal part consists of the embolus, through which runs the ejaculating duct, and the conductor, or protector of the tip of the embolus. Various projections or apophyses are usually present, the most important of which arises from the tibia.

This tibial apophysis is received by a special groove in the female epigyne (Fig. 22) and helps to secure the union of the two organs. The process of mating is described in a later chapter.

It is clear that one consequence of the complexity of the palpal organs and the epigyne is the difficulty or impossibility of cross-breeding between two different species. The shapes and sizes of all the parts of the tarsal organ are characteristics of each different species of male spider and are therefore very helpful details when a spider is being examined in order to determine its name. The female epigyne is so constructed that it receives the palp accurately and securely, but clearly the different palp of another species will not be effective. Thus hybrids are virtually unknown among spiders.

The legs of spiders are among their most active and versatile organs, responsible for much more than mere walking. Though of very different lengths they are otherwise remarkably uniform in construction throughout the order.

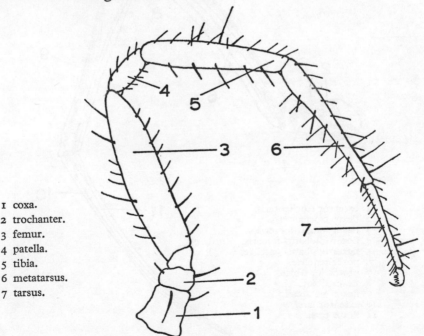

1 coxa.
2 trochanter.
3 femur.
4 patella.
5 tibia.
6 metatarsus.
7 tarsus.

Figure 7. Leg of a spider.

Each leg consists of seven segments, coxa, trochanter, femur, patella, tibia, metatarsus and tarsus (Fig. 7), that is to say the same segments as a pedipalp with the insertion of a metatarsus. Each segment is a chitinous tube containing muscles, the arrangement of which is shown in Fig. 8, nerves, and blood. The coxal segments never have gnathobases, such as are sometimes found on the anterior legs of other arachnids; they lie symmetrically grouped round the sternum and are normally immovable, though all the other segments have various degrees of freedom. The tarsus always ends in claws. These are two or three in number, either smooth or toothed like a comb, and the general rule is that hunting spiders have two claws,

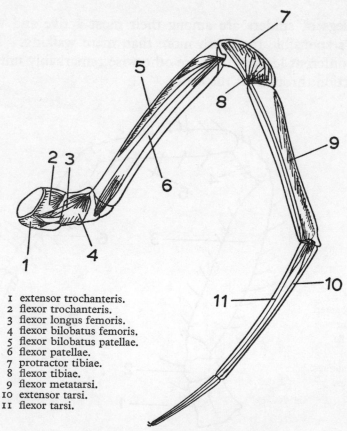

1　extensor trochanteris.
2　flexor trochanteris.
3　flexor longus femoris.
4　flexor bilobatus femoris.
5　flexor bilobatus patellae.
6　flexor patellae.
7　protractor tibiae.
8　flexor tibiae.
9　flexor metatarsi.
10　extensor tarsi.
11　flexor tarsi.

Figure 8.　Leg-muscles of a spider.

while the web-spinners possess a small, median, third claw in addition. In some families the end of the tarsus also has two groups of setae known as ungual tufts.

The spines and setae with which the legs are clothed form an important part of a spider's sensory equipment. These are of several kinds. The stoutest are spines, which rise from a cup-like modification of the leg-segment, within which their base is broadened by a ring of chitin. They are dark-coloured on the outside and lighter within, so that when seen under the microscope they give the impression that they are hollow. They are present in small numbers on each leg-segment, where their positions are constant for each species, genus or family, so that their arrangement is often used in classification.

By contrast the setae are not so strong, though fundamentally similar. They have no cupule on the chitin, but arise more directly from the surface. They are present in very large numbers so that they cover an area and give it a hirsute appearance.

The finest and relatively longest are known as trichobothria. They are usually confined to the tarsus and metatarsus and are believed to respond to sound waves, so that they act as a spider's ears. More accurately, therefore, a spider may be said to feel a sound; in fact, all spines and setae are tactile organs, supplementing the spider's poor vision by an amazingly delicate sense of touch.

As has been said, the only appendages of the opisthosoma are the spinnerets, which are found in no other order of the Arachnida, and which belong to the tenth and eleventh somites. On the tenth somite the exopodites alone exist and are called the anterior pair of spinnerets, on the eleventh the small endopodites are the median and the larger exopodites are the posterior spinnerets. Each spinneret is a short cylindrical appendage of one, two or three segments: the tip is squarely or obliquely cut off to form the spinning-field on which are most of the actual tubes through which the silk issues. These are of two kinds, spools and spigots (Fig. 9). The former are minute and are scattered, to the number of sixty to a hundred, over the field; the latter are larger, with seldom more than five to a single spinneret, and constant in number and position.

Each silk gland in the abdomen is connected by its ducts to its own spool or spigot.

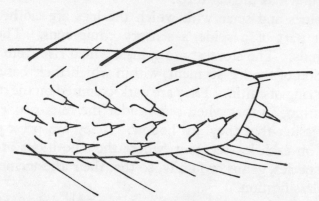

Figure 9. One spinneret, showing silk-producing spools.

In certain families of spiders the endopodites of the tenth somite are represented by an organ called the cribellum or little sieve. This is an ovoid area of the cuticle perforated by a large number of small holes, each of which is supplied with its own duct from the cribellum glands. The silk which exudes is drawn out by a special comb, a row of spines on the metatarsus of the fourth legs known as the calamistrum (Fig. 10). This carded silk is laid down on a base of ordinary threads and has a characteristic bluish colour and a rough, untidy appearance. It is very commonly seen in the webs that are spun from keyholes, from cracks in gate posts and in the corners of shed windows. Arachnologists are uncertain as to whether they should put all families of cribellate spiders together in a group, or whether they should be distributed so as to come nearer to the families which, save for the cribellum, they otherwise resemble. The arguments will not be discussed here; the problem, which is complicated by the possibility of converging evolution, has been mentioned because it is an excellent example of the differences between the points of view of the evolutionary taxonomist, who wishes his systems to represent the paths of evolution, and the classifier, who only wants a practical scheme which will make easier the task of identification. It is a simple matter to see if a given spider has a cribellum, without worrying about the way in which it acquired it.

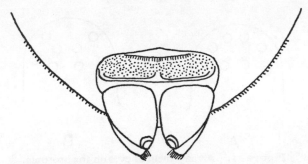

Figure 10. Cribellum and spinnerets of the spider Ciniflo.

There remain for consideration the external sense-organs. In addition to the setae described above, these are the eyes, the lyriform organs and the tarsal organs (Figs. 13 and 14).

In all spiders the eyes are simple ocelli (Fig. 11), unlike the compound, faceted, eyes of the crayfish or the house-fly. They are usually placed on the forepart of the carapace, but in some families they are raised on more or less conspicuous eminences. Nearly always they are eight in number; there are never more than eight, but in several genera they are reduced to six, four or two. Some cave-dwelling spiders are eyeless.

It is the custom to describe the normal eight eyes as being arranged in two transverse rows and to distinguish median and lateral eyes in each row. The anterior median eyes are sometimes called the direct eyes. The curvature of the rows, which may have a convexity forwards ("recurved") or a convexity backwards ("procurved"), and the distances between individual eyes are characteristics much used in classification. Individual abnormalities in eye-pattern, involving missing eyes, are not rare.

In outward appearance a spider's eye is a smooth circular spot of the exoskeleton, free from pigment and shaped to form a convex lens. Most eyes look black, but some are pearly white, a difference responsible for the old naming of diurnal and nocturnal eyes, but there is little evidence for the different functions which this suggests. Beneath the lens, which is shed when the spider moults, lies the epidermis, and under this are the visual cells of the retina, in connexion with the optic nerve (Fig. 12).

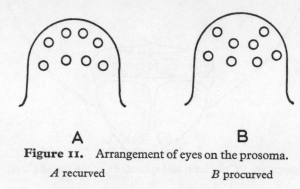

A   **B**

Figure 11.   Arrangement of eyes on the prosoma.

A recurved   *B* procurved

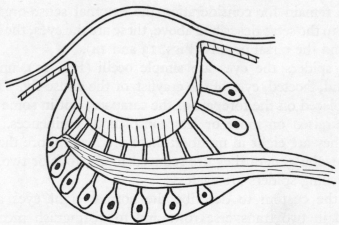

Figure 12.   Section through the eye of a spider (diagrammatic).

Spiders have very different powers of vision. To web-spinners, which rely almost entirely on the vibrations of the threads of their webs, the eyes have only a secondary importance. They seem to form significant images of objects within about half an inch of the spider's head, but not of objects further away than this. They undoubtedly respond to moving objects more readily than to stationary ones. Very possibly their chief value is to distinguish between daylight and darkness.

Hunting and jumping spiders, on the contrary, have larger eyes and depend far more on the keenness of their eyesight. It has long been known that they appear to recognize prey or mates at distances of eight to ten inches. Investigation by Homann of Göttingen (1934) has shown us the different parts played by different eyes when a jumping spider sees and leaps upon an insect. These differences were revealed by a successful method of covering one or more eyes with a blindfold of black wax, a technique which enables us to break down the apparently continuous process into its separate reflex actions.

The normal sequence is as follows:

i. An image of the prey is formed by one of the posterior lateral eyes, which have a wide angle of vision, but there is no response by the spider if the insect remains stationary.

ii. If it moves, the spider turns and the image is formed on an anterior lateral eye, but if this eye is blindfolded no further action takes place.

iii. Normally, however, turning continues, bringing into existence images on all four eyes of the anterior row. The images on the two anterior lateral eyes produce a form of binocular vision and perception of distance. The spider begins to creep towards the object.

iv. A closer approach results in better definition in the anterior median eyes. Courtship may begin if the object is another jumping spider; if it is not the spider's approach changes to a "stalking" by very slow forward creeping.

v. At about 1.5 cm. distance, the spider leaps upon and bites its victim.

It is thus revealed that each pair of eyes has a special function and that the spider responds appropriately to the stimuli from them. What appears in nature to be a continuous process can be broken down, with the help of a few spots of black wax, into a series or chain of separate reflex actions.

The posterior median eyes are not involved in hunting: they receive impressions from objects in the rear.

The lyriform organs (Fig. 13) are the most mysterious and elusive of a spider's sensory equipment.

They appear under a microscope as slit-like incisions in the exoskeleton, arranged singly or in groups, with almost a hundred such groups on legs, carapace and sternum. It has been suggested, without much experimental support, that they are auditory organs, scent organs, organs of muscular tension and detectors of atmospheric moisture. Most recent opinion, backed by experiment, suggests that they are organs of chemo-reception. This is a way of saying that they react to vapour of what may appear to human beings to be odorous substances.

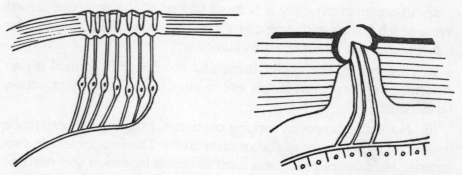

Figure 13. Diagram of a lyriform organ in the exoskeleton.   **Figure 14.** Diagram of a tarsal organ.

The tarsal organs (Fig. 14) are also chemo-receptors and their use has been satisfactorily demonstrated by Blumenthal (1935). These organs can be seen under the microscope as small round holes in the upper surface of the tarsus, leading into a depression at the bottom of which lies a small projection. They are used in the testing of drinking-water and the examination of edible prey. If the tarsus of one of the anterior legs of a thirsty spider is touched with a drop of water, the spider moves forward and drinks; if one of the posterior legs be so touched, the spider turns round and drinks. If the tarsal organ is sealed these responses disappear, and if a drop of water touches any other joint of the leg, the spider merely moves away. Blumenthal also showed that the organ enabled a spider to distinguish between water, brine, sugar solution and quinine.

3 *Internal Organs and Physiology*

FOR describing the internal structure of a spider there is no better method than the simple one of treating it as a collection of systems of organs—alimentary, vascular, respiratory, nervous, excretory, gonadial and glandular—and combining an account of the parts themselves with their physiology or functionings.

Alimentary System.   The alimentary canal follows the arthropod pattern of conveniently dividing itself into fore-gut or stomodaeum, mid-gut or intestine, and hind-gut or proctodaeum. The first and the last of these are lined with chitin, epidermal invaginations of the exoskeleton.

The mouth is a very small aperture between the lip, already mentioned, and the rostrum just above it.   It leads into the pharynx, which is a narrow channel formed from opposed grooves in two chitinous plates, the epipharynx and the hypopharynx (Fig. 15). From its inner end a curved tube, the oesophagus, unites pharynx and sucking stomach.   The latter is a heart-shaped widening of the canal, lying on the endosternite, its upper surface attached by muscles to the carapace above.   The contraction of these muscles increases the volume of the stomach and so causes it to suck the liquid food up the pharynx and through the oesophagus.   It has none of the digestive functions of a true stomach.   Here ends the fore-gut.

The mid-gut or mesenteron is a soft tube directed towards the

B

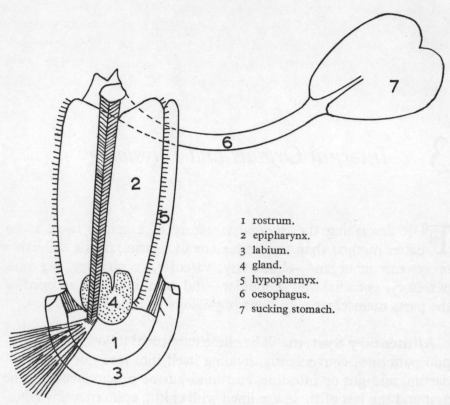

1 rostrum.
2 epipharynx.
3 labium.
4 gland.
5 hypopharynx.
6 oesophagus.
7 sucking stomach.

Figure 15. Fore-gut of a spider.

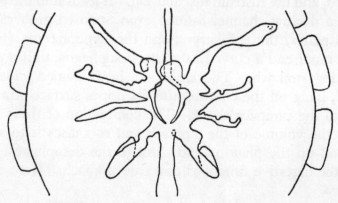

Figure 16. Intestinal diverticula of a spider.

pedicel and giving off two lateral diverticula which lie in the pro-soma on each side of the mesenteron itself. From them secondary caeca lead towards the legs and may enter the coxae. This arrange-ment (Fig. 16) gives the mid-gut a very large volume and helps it to retain and digest a large quantity of fluid. The mesenteron then enters the opisthosoma, widens, and gives off four lateral tubes which branch into an extensive system of diverticula, filling a large part of the cavity or haemocoel of the opisthosoma. These diverti-cula, often vaguely referred to as the "liver", act as possible storage space for further quantities of food, which is slowly digested and absorbed from them.

Finally, the mid-gut passes into the hind-gut or proctodaeum, which is characterized by a small dorsal caecum, the stercoral pocket. Faecal matter accumulates in this pocket and is ejected through a short, straight rectum, at intervals or when the spider is startled.

It will be appreciated by those familiar with the crayfish and the cockroach that the spider has a very characteristic form of alimen-tary canal. The lateral diverticula in the prosoma and the so-called liver in the opisthosoma are much more highly developed than are the corresponding devices which increase the absorptive area of the canal in other arthropods. The result is that a spider can take in a considerable quantity of food whenever it happens to be available.

A spider's food is always liquid. Spiders feed chiefly on insects, and when captured the insect is held between the maxillary lobes of the pedipalpi. Digestive glands within these lobes secrete enzyme-carrying fluid upon it, and the chemical changes which constitute digestion begin outside the spider's body. The resulting solution is sucked in by the action of the stomach.

The oesophagus contains taste-organs. Experiments have made it clear that, wide as is the choice of possible food, there is much that a spider appears to dislike and much that it refuses to eat at all. In such cases the spider drops the insect or prey, produces from its maxillary glands a copious secretion which washes the oesophagus and adjacent organs, and finally removes the distasteful material by rubbing its mouth-parts on the ground, or on a leaf, or brushing them with its pedipalpi.

The large amount of food which can be imbibed by a hungry spider in favourable circumstances causes its abdomen to swell in a way seen but rarely in insects or crustaceans. The slow digesting of the material in the diverticula means, of course, that a long time may elapse before another meal becomes a necessity. This is a valuable adaptation. Web-spinning spiders have to rely very largely on the chances that may bring an insect into their webs, so that perhaps more than most other arthropods they can meet with confidence the familiar question, "Shall I dine today—or not?" a question to which the environment's answer is "Probably not." That spiders can survive long periods without a meal has been known for many years. Blackwall in 1829-31 recorded a fast of twenty months in a small British Theridiid species, and a hundred years later Baerg noted that large mygalomorph spiders survived for more than two years without feeding.

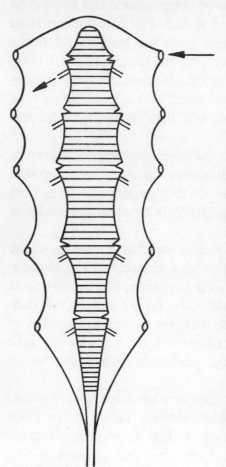

Figure 17. Heart of a spider in pericardium.

Vascular System. The spider's body cavity is a haemocoel, that is to say its internal organs are all surrounded with blood. The blood is a colourless fluid, alkaline in reaction. It soon clots in the open air. It contains various amoeboid corpuscles, but is said to be free from any respiratory pigments such as haemocyanin.

The heart (Fig. 17) is similar to the heart of a cockroach, but it is limited to the opisthosoma, where it lies centrally, just below the dorsal cuticle. It is an elongated tube, narrowing posteriorly, with a pericardium into which it opens by two to five pairs of cardiac ostia. From its front end the anterior artery or aorta passes through the pedicel and, branching, supplies blood to the muscles and nerve ganglia of the prosoma. The organs of the opisthosoma are supplied from two or three pairs of lateral arteries and by a posterior artery from the tip of the heart.

The blood which has flowed from the heart through these vessels collects in sinuses, from which it passes into the leaves of the lung-books (Fig. 18). Here it absorbs oxygen and is returned by the pressure of the heart-beat to the pericardium. The rate of beating varies considerably in different families of spiders, being as low as 26 beats per minute in some, and as high as 150 per minute in others. The system seems to be rather inefficient, for one of the most surprising things about spiders is the way in which they become quite exhausted if compelled to run rapidly for a minute or so.

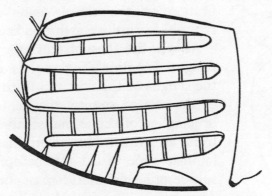

Figure 18. Diagram of a lung-book, showing only four leaves.

Respiratory System. Two methods of oxygenating the tissues are to be found among spiders. In the most primitive families there are two pairs of lung-books. These are large hollow spaces in the forepart of the opisthosoma, communicating with the outside air through small pores. They are clearly distinguishable as pale-coloured patches on the lower surface. Inside each lung-book there are about twenty hollow leaves, folds of the body-wall, in communication with the sinuses. Blood from the sinuses enters the leaves and is oxygenated by diffusion through their surfaces, losing carbon dioxide in the same way.

In most families of spiders there is one pair of lung-books, their action supplemented by tracheae. These are fine tubes, similar to the tracheae of insects, but they do not branch so freely. Only in a few families do the tracheae reach the prosoma and legs; in general they are confined to the opisthosoma, where they ramify among the liver-diverticula and the silk-glands, the places, in fact, where the blood-vessels are sparse. In the tracheae oxygen passes directly to the tissues.

In a few families of small spiders there are no lung-books and all respiration is tracheal.

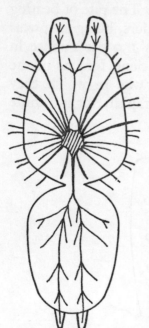

Figure 19. Nervous system of a spider.

Nervous System. The nervous system of spiders represents a very considerable modification of the simple ganglionated chain typical of primitive arthropods.

Above the oesophagus the supra-oesophageal ganglion (Fig. 19) is derived from the ganglia of the first and third somites, that of the second somite, the deuterocerebrum, or ganglion of the second somite being absent from all Arachnida. Commissures of the familiar type circle the oesophagus to the sub-oesophageal nerve-mass below the endosternite. This is a thin plate of chitin in the prosoma, the largest single item in a spider's rudimentary endo-skeleton. From this lower nerve centre, whose separate ganglia can just be detected, there radiates a series of small blood-vessels, which supply it from the aorta. The maximum number of these ganglia is seventeen, five belonging to the prosoma and twelve which during development have travelled forward along the nerve cord to join the sternal nerve centre.

Five pairs of nerves from the prosomatic ganglia supply the pedipalpi and the legs. The nerve cord passes through the pedicel and, on entering the opisthosoma, divides into two parallel branches, from which nerves arise metamerically to supply the various regions and organs of the opisthosoma.

Excretory System. This system consists of two separate portions, the coxal glands and the Malpighian tubules.

The coxal glands are coelomoducts, that is to say they have been developed from paired tubes which grow out from the walls of the coelom to the exterior. In some animals they become genital ducts, in others excretory, and in many arachnids they form a fully-developed excretory system. In spiders they are much reduced, and the gland on each side consists, at the most, of four parts, known as the sacculus, the collecting canal, and the excretory canal. This last has openings on the coxae of the first and third legs (Fig. 20A). In some families of spiders, each coxal gland consists of the sacculus only, with an orifice on the coxa of the pedipalp (Fig. 20B).

The Malpighian tubules arise in varying numbers from the hind end of the mid-gut, and ramify among the diverticula of the intestine. They absorb excretory matter from the haemocoel and pass it out through the rectum.

Reproductive System. The sexes are always separate in spiders, and the male system is very simple. Two elongated ovoid testes lie in the opisthosoma below the intestine; their anterior ends lead directly to a pair of tubes, the vasa deferentia, which, curving downwards, unite to form a common duct. This opens, as already mentioned, at a very small orifice in the middle of the second opisthosomatic sternite.

The ovaries are, similarly, two ovoid bodies in positions which correspond to those of the testes, but they are larger and show seasonal variation (Fig. 21). When the ova are mature the ovaries fill the bulk of the opisthosoma, compressing the other organs

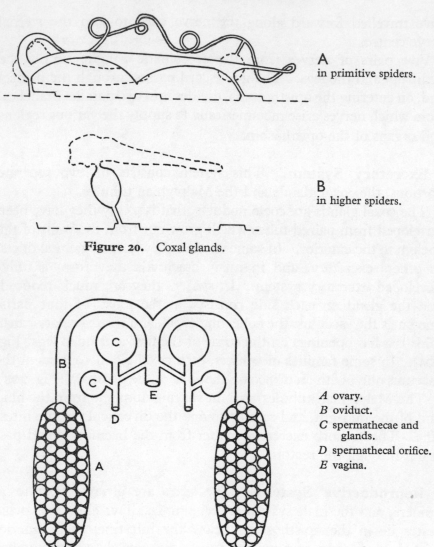

A
in primitive spiders.

B
in higher spiders.

Figure 20.   Coxal glands.

A ovary.
B oviduct.
C spermathecae and
glands.
D spermathecal orifice.
E vagina.

Figure 21.   Reproductive system of a female spider.

therein.   As is usual among the Arthropoda, the ovaries are continuous with the oviducts, two broad tubes which, like the vasa
deferentia, curve downwards and meet to form a central vagina.
Through the vagina the eggs are laid.   From its sides there arise two
lateral ducts, leading to the spermathecae and their associated

glands. The spermatozoa from the male are stored in the spermathecae and fertilize the eggs as they pass down the vagina.

Vagina and spermathecae and glands lie within and just above a characteristic genital area known as the epigyne or epigynum (Fig. 22). The outward appearance of this area is affected by the sizes, shapes and visibility of the glands and ducts below the surface and is recognizably different in all different species so that illustrations of it have been used for many years as the surest way to designate or to identify a given specimen of a mature female spider. In addition to the glands and ducts mentioned above, the epigyne often contains special provision for accommodating the conductor of the male pedipalp during mating.

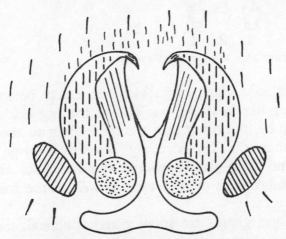

Figure 22. Epigyne of female spider.

Silk-producing System. The abdomen also contains the silk-glands, undoubtedly the most characteristic organs in the spider's body (Fig. 23). At least seven or eight different kinds of glands have been described as a result of many dissections, and, as far as our knowledge goes at present, it seems probable that the silk-producing systems are appreciably different in the different groups of families. There are, however, four recognizable forms of glands which, it seems, are present in all spiders. They are named the ampullaceal, cylindrical, aciniform and piriform glands.

B*

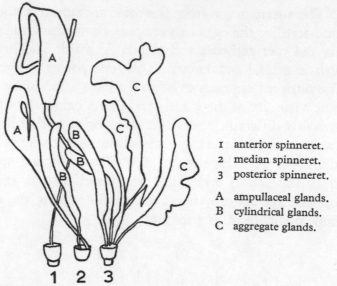

1 anterior spinneret.
2 median spinneret.
3 posterior spinneret.

A ampullaceal glands.
B cylindrical glands.
C aggregate glands.

Figure 23.   Silk glands of a spider.

The ampullaceal glands, of which there may be as many as a dozen, are egg-like in shape, one end of the egg being drawn out into a long tube, the other into a duct leading to the anterior or median spinnerets. The swelling contains a large reserve of liquid silk, and these glands produce the drag-line, which spiders lay down behind them as they run, as well as the frame and the radii of orb-webs.

The aciniform glands are smaller and spherical; they are very numerous, and their ducts open on the median or posterior spinnerets. Their silk is used in cocoon-making. The cylindrical glands, six in number, produce the coloured wadding often found round the egg-mass inside the cocoon, and in consequence they do not occur in male spiders.

The piriform glands, which are perhaps only a modification of the aciniform, are used to make the "attachment discs" or bands of short threads which at intervals secure a long drag-line to its base.

In addition to these, the cribellum has a number of small glands of its own, and in certain families there are aggregate glands, whose secretion forms the adhesive droplets on the threads of the web.

4 Life-History

ALL spiders hatch from eggs, and all spiders' eggs are small, spherical, usually cream-coloured or yellow, and are contained in a cocoon of silk in numbers that range between two and a thousand or more. The eggs develop at speeds that are determined in part by the nature of the species and in part by the temperature. In the temperate zones of the world there are many species that produce the first cocoon of eggs in the early summer; they hatch in a few weeks and another cocoonful follows them later in the year. Other species of spiders, which mature in the autumn, lay their eggs before the winter and then die. These eggs develop slowly, and the young appear in the following spring. Some species have overlapping life-cycles, so that both adults and young can be found at all seasons; and a few live for several years and produce a family annually.

During their embryonic development spiders undergo a curious transformation known as reversion (Fig. 24). This is a change from a position in which the dorsal surface of the body is concave to one in which it is convex and more closely resembles the adult. In due time the egg-membrane or chorion is broken with the help of a sharp point or egg-tooth on each chelicera, and there emerges a small spider. Since it is so like the adult in all essentials save size and sexual maturity it is known as a nymph and not as a larva.

At first it scarcely moves; it neither spins nor feeds, but lives on the store of yolk still present in its alimentary canal. It has no teeth on its chelicerae, smooth claws on its tarsi, and no pigment in its cuticle. All the members of a cocoon live together, usually within the cocoon-case, where the first moult or casting of the exoskeleton often takes place.

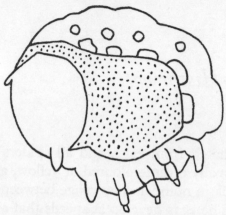

Figure 24. Embryo of a spider, before reversion.

In the course of one or two moultings the small spider develops all the vital powers, save that of reproduction. It can spin silk and catch its own food; a tendency to prey on its own kind, a cannibalism which lasts all its life, appears; so that the young spiders disperse and lead an independent existence, increasing in size by periodic moultings until they become adult.

One of the unexpected features of the early life of spiders is the fact that the escape from the cocoon does not always take place at the same developmental stage, but varies among the different families, and may occur before or after the first moult.

The dispersal of recently-hatched spiders, mentioned above as a necessary consequence of their cannibalistic nature, is often unnoticed but is sometimes spectacular. Many spiders, like scorpions, do not undertake any obvious dispersing activities; they wander, more or less by chance, in various directions, avoiding each other and thus scattering themselves over an area which is not unduly extensive. There is room for a lot of spiders in half an acre.

However, the spider's most characteristic method of dispersal by floating through the air on a silk thread is a phenomenon which has been known for a very long time. This thread has been given the name of gossamer, and has attracted the attention of poets and writers of all kinds, who have otherwise taken no interest in the life of the spider.

There is sufficient peculiarity about the actions of the small spider itself. The stimulus to fly seems to come at least in part from the state of the weather, for gossamer is most often seen on warm days in spring, and all accounts of great abundance of these floating threads have stressed the calm brightness of the day. The spider's action is first to climb, and it crawls, often laboriously enough, up a plant-stem, railing or gate-post, until it gets to the top. Here it turns its body so that it is facing the direction from which the breeze is blowing, and thus orientated, raises its abdomen (Fig. 25). It now secretes a small drop of silk from its ampullaceal glands, and the silk is carried away by the breeze, producing the tension which converts the silk from the fluid form, in which it exists in the glands, into the solid elastic thread, which is found outside. This remarkable chemical property of silk is further described in Chapter 6.

As more and more silk is thus drawn from the spider, the thread becomes longer and longer, drags more and more strongly until the spider floats up and away.

This is obviously a method of dispersal that cannot be controlled, and the length of the journey is determined by chance. Records, often quoted, from ships on which spiders have come to rest, have given two hundred miles as the distance which the aeronaut must have been carried from the nearest land. A study of the spiders that are found on oceanic islands makes it probable that many of them have arrived in this way, and have established themselves.

One aspect of gossamer flight concerns the identities of the species that undertake it. A number, not large enough, of observers have collected "gossamer spiders" both in Europe and America, and about a hundred different species have been identified among them. It is believed that some species, at least, of nearly every family may

adopt aerial travel at some stage in their lives. The largest spiders
are, of course, too heavy to fly, but among the small species adults
have been found on floating threads. The whole phenomenon
calls for more investigation.

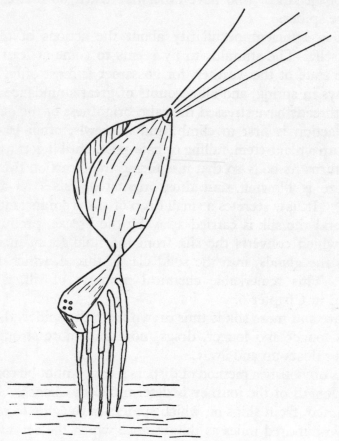

Figure 25. Young spider about to "fly".

Related to gossamer-flight though distinct from it is the fact,
which may be mentioned here, that spiders form a proportion of
the drifting organisms, known as aerial plankton, which rises to a
height of at least 14,000 feet. Figures published by Coad in 1930
showed that above an area of a square mile there may be floating
from twelve to thirty million arthropods of various kinds.

Established in its new home, the young spider must feed itself, in consequence of which it will grow. The growth of spiders, like the growth of crabs, is discontinuous, because the animal is surrounded by a hard protective coat, largely of inanimate chitin. This exoskeleton is cast, or moulted, at intervals, the correct name for the process being ecdysis. Thus the growth of a spider may be pictured as consisting of an increase in the number of cells within an almost inelastic case. Immediately after freedom from this there is a short period of rapid increase in size, until the new skeleton hardens and the process starts all over again. This is a very different method of growth from that shown by most animals, and the overall difference is shown at Fig. 26.

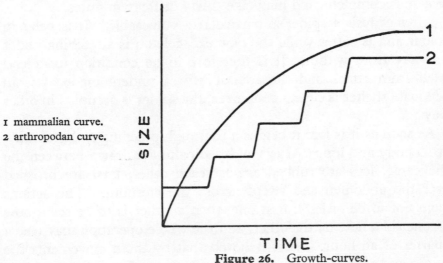

1 mammalian curve.
2 arthropodan curve.

TIME

Figure 26. Growth-curves.

The operation of casting the skin is one of complexity and not a little danger, and must not be thought of as a mere bursting by pressure of a coat that has become too tight. There are changes within, which help to prepare the animal for the action it is about to undertake, and in captive spiders it can easily be seen that the appetite vanishes and the legs darken in colour. The silk, too, becomes viscous, and does not flow readily from the spinnerets.

For the actual process of moulting the spider finds a place where it can hang upside down from a number of threads which it spins specially for this purpose. As it hangs, a split appears along the front of the carapace, just above the chelicerae, spreads round the edges just above the legs, so that the shield of the prosoma lifts off, except at its hinder end. The cuticle of the opisthosoma splits from the pedicel to the spinnerets, and allows the body within to emerge without difficulty.

The longest and most serious part of the process is the pulling out of the legs and palpi. The spider still hangs from its tarsal claws, and it undertakes an almost continuous series of heaving, stretching and pulling movements each one of which drags the whole set of ten appendages a fraction of a millimetre from their old cases. A total of five or six hundred pulls may be needed before release is complete, and may take thirty or forty minutes.

After ecdysis a spider is particularly vulnerable. It is paler in colour and is softer while the new exoskeleton is stretching under pressure from within. It is therefore in no condition to defend itself from attack and the advisability of undergoing ecdysis in adequate shelter is clear. Moreover, the spider is occupied in other ways.

As soon as it is free it begins a thorough preening and grooming of its body and limbs. Legs and pedipalpi are drawn between the chelicerae, legs are rubbed against each other, tarsi are brushed over the abdomen and swept across the sternum. The actions seem not to be orderly: first one, then another is to be seen, now on one side, now on the other, and the whole operation may take a quarter of an hour. It is believed that by these movements the spines and setae are set in the best directions; but whether this is true or not it is only one instance of the general grooming of the body which spiders constantly perform.

The procedure may be induced by dropping a house-spider into a basin of water. It does not sink, but swims or sculls across the surface until it can climb out or is rescued. If it is then returned to its web, it can be watched thoroughly drying itself by this method. Again, after a meal a spider often draws its palpi and perhaps its forelegs between its chelicerae. It appears to be important for the individual that its body be kept clean. The exoskeleton carries various sense-organs, which cannot function efficiently if they are clogged with dust. A few spiders have special groups of bristles which act very effectively as combs, and it is surprising that there are not more of these adaptations. Care for personal cleanliness is one of the safety-devices in spiders that may be regarded as adaptations that help towards survival; and the grooming or preening just described has been seen in most of the other orders of arachnids. It is probably universal.

Many spiders show a habit which is often described as "shamming dead", and which evidently has a survival value since many predators are attracted by moving prey and pay no attention to stationary objects. The condition of the spider is one in which the legs are drawn in, close to the body; it lies quite motionless and under examination often permits itself to be passed from hand to hand with no sign of life.

Among web-spiders this condition of insensitivity or catalepsy often follows a drop from the web into the sanctuary of the less accessible regions of the undergrowth. "Drop" is perhaps too passive a word, for the spider can be seen to apply its spinnerets to its support and then to kick itself downwards instead of lightly falling. This initial force provides the tension that causes the solidification of the liquid silk; a useful precaution since, when danger is past, the thread enables the spider to regain its web. Observation shows that some species are far more sensitive than others and are inclined to drop at the slightest provocation.

A very valuable feature of a spider's life is its ability to shed its legs when necessary, for it may be supposed that the spiders' chief enemies, birds, may sometimes seize a leg when making an attempt to seize the body. At once the leg separates at the coxa-trochanter articulation, and the spider has a chance to escape on the remaining seven. By experiment, using forceps to replace the beak of a bird, it is found that if a leg is seized by the femur, separation is almost immediate; if a tarsus is grasped the spider may turn round, push with its other legs against the points of the forceps and, rather more slowly, wrench itself free. This is called autotomy and a characteristic to be emphasized is that the breaking of the leg always occurs at the same place. Here not only are the connecting tissues weakest, but there is also provision to avoid excessive loss of blood. If a leg is cut through the middle of the femur with a pair of scissors, the spider is unlikely to survive: and if a leg is injured the spider usually pulls it off and is better without it.

This autotomy is associated with a spider's power of regeneration. The power to replace lost parts is widespread among animals of many kinds; in general it is an ability that has grown less as evolution has proceeded. It is almost unlimited among the Coelenterata and the Planarians; among vertebrates the regrowth of a lizard's tail is the most conspicuous and almost the only example.

Among spiders a new leg grows under the scar of the one that has been lost, and at the next ecdysis it is set free with the rest. Extensive research on this regeneration, carried out by Professor P. Bonnet, has shown that a certain minimum time, about two-thirds of the interval between successive moults, is needed if the new leg is to be comparable in size to its fellow: if the loss occurs later than this, or nearer to the time of moulting, an undersized limb is the result. This explains the asymmetry of legs which individual spiders often show.

Power of regeneration is not confined to the legs, for chelicerae, palpi and spinnerets can all be replaced if they are lost. More than one leg can be restored at the same time. In the extreme case, Bonnet experimented with spiders that had shed all eight legs. Such limbless bodies could not, of course, have survived in nature, but in his laboratory they were cradled in cotton wool, placed near water which they could drink, and fed with flies offered to them in forceps. In due course they all moulted and appeared with complete sets of eight legs.

The life of a spider, as outlined in this chapter, appears as the life of an individual almost wholly concerned with survival among ever-present dangers. These day-to-day or minute-to-minute actions can be collectively described as maintenance behaviour, much of which can be accurately described or analysed as reflex action.

Reflex actions, which are well known in all animals including man, are sometimes found to occur in a connected series, each unit in which is an invariable response to a particular stimulus, the whole chain taking on the outward appearance of a correlated, purposeful act. An example of such a chain reflex was given in the description of the jumping spider's attack on a nearby insect. Another example is a similar chain, which was described many years ago and in which a continuing series of actions has been split into its component reflexes and the stimulus for each determined.

Professor H. Peters (1931) analysed the capture of a fly by a garden-spider into five parts, as follows:

i. *Movement towards Prey.* The stimulus is the sudden movement of the web and the direction of movement is determined by the vibrations of the threads.

ii. *The Long Bite.* The stimulus is the struggle of the entangled insect: immobile objects are not bitten.

iii. *The Enshrouding.* The stimulus is a chemo-tactic one, received when the legs and palpi touch the victim.

iv. *The Short Bite.* The stimulus is received from the silk covering of the trussed insect.

v. *The Carrying.* The stimulus is a chemical one, received from the short bite.

The operation can be started at any point by giving a spider a live, an unwrapped or a wrapped fly.

From these and similar analyses among other animals there arises an attempt to explain all behaviour in terms of reflexes, the implication of which is that all the actions of an animal are inevitable responses to stimuli and that the animal itself is no more than a living machine. Such an idea is characteristic of what is known as mechanistic biology: it does not receive universal acceptance for it leads to an over-simplified explanation of vital phenomena. The instinctive behaviour of an animal is more complicated than this.

5   *The Reproductive Cycle*

THE reproductive habits of spiders are so unusual that they deserve a separate chapter: they form a characteristic part of the biology of spiders, and also provide a very good example of instinctive behaviour.

As has been said, male spiders are indistinguishable from females while they are immature, and it is only after the penultimate moult that they betray their sex by the swelling of the palpal tarsi. At this period their behaviour does not differ from their behaviour in their younger days: sub-adult males kept under observation have given no evidence of forthcoming change, spinning webs and catching flies as before. Finally they moult.

The appearance of the complete tarsal organ, though it signifies physical maturity, does not, however, coincide with an immediate change of habit. For some days life continues as before, until the spider takes its first essential step. The palpal organs are fully formed, but they contain no spermatozoa, for these are produced in the opisthosoma, and the orifice of the vasa deferentia on the lower side of the second opisthosomatic somite is beyond the direct reach of the short pedipalpi.

The operation now undertaken to overcome this difficulty is called sperm-induction. The spider spins a small web, the sperm-web (Fig. 27), square or triangular in shape, and inclined or almost vertical: upon this he shakes or rubs his opisthosoma, depositing thus a drop of semen. Into this drop the pedipalpi are dipped, one after the other or, more rarely, together, the fluid is drawn in by capillarity, and the pedipalpi are thus charged and made ready for use. The process occupies from five to twenty-five minutes: it is the step that marks final maturity and in some species induction is performed before the female has been sought. Among other species of spiders it is included in the courtship, either early or late in the ceremony; and by others again it is quickly repeated if unions are numerous or prolonged.

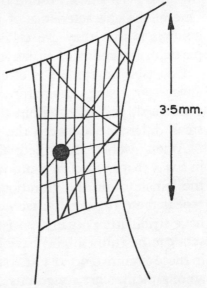

Male web-spiders henceforward cease to spin webs and change their mode of life. Driven by stimuli for which hormones are probably responsible, they wander with the outward appearance of being in search of a female. There

Figure 27. Sperm web of crab-spider, *Xysticus cristatus.*

seems to be no evidence to suggest that the finding of a mature female of the same species is directed or governed by anything other than chance.

This is a point of vital importance in the biology of web-spiders: it is of much less consequence to the active, hunting species. By abandoning its web the male spider has sacrificed all chance of feeding again and has entered upon a far more strenuous life than that to which it had previously become accustomed. However, sooner or later it encounters the stimuli that determine its next set of actions, to which the name courtship is applied.

It may be that the male sees the female, or it may be that his tarsi touch the threads on the outskirts of her web, or brush against some threads that she has spun. There is no doubt that tactile or chemo-tactile stimuli, separately or sometimes together, are responsible for at least the beginning of the act of courtship. Spiders in laboratories have been known to begin these activities at the sight of another male, at the sight of their own mirror-image, at contact with the cast skin or the autotomized leg of a female, or with sand that had been shaken round the cage in which a female was living. One of the characteristics of instinctive actions in many kinds of animals is that they are called into existence in response to one particular stimulus or situation, and in no other way.

Courtship in spiders is often elaborate and prolonged, and it is always surprising. Its nature depends on the nature of the spiders concerned, and even within the limits of a single genus there are small differences between the species.

Among web-spiders the male often pulls at the edge of the web in a way that must clearly produce vibrations which do not stimulate the female as do the vibrations of a captured fly. The male may repeat these tugs at the web as he walks along it. Some species have stridulating organs consisting of ridges against which a special seta can be rubbed, and have been seen to bring these into action in these circumstances. Others, the common house spider Tegenaria among them, start a vigorous drumming with their palpi upon the sheet of the web, and they keep up this drumming as they cautiously move across the web until their outstretched forelegs touch those of the female. Wandering spiders are often content merely to crawl over one another, their tarsi tickling their bodies as they do so, but wolf-spiders and jumping spiders are more spectacular. The following is a description of the courtship of the common woodland wolf-spider, *Lycosa lugubris*.

The male stops in front of the female and raises his body on six posterior legs: he lifts first one palp and then the other until they are vertical and shoots out his forelegs sideways. This remarkable position is retained for a few seconds only; then, while the front legs move or wave more obviously, the palpi drop to their usual places. Again there is a momentary pause, then the movement of the legs stops, one palp is raised, then the other, and the pose is held once more (Fig. 28).

These actions are continued twenty, thirty, perhaps forty times. As a rule both spiders remain stationary, two or three centimetres apart. The female, quiescent, appears to be watching the male;

I have never seen her attack him. Then, suddenly, the male stops, relaxes his legs so that his body drops to the ground, and now runs crabwise round the female, the tarsi of his front legs in contact with her body and limbs as he circles. He seldom makes more than two circuits before he climbs on to her back.

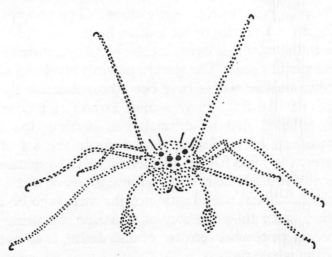

Figure 28. Courtship pose of *Lycosa lugubris*; a wolf spider.

Although a very large number of descriptions of the courtship of different species have been written and published, their various authors are not agreed as to the cause and actual function of these remarkable actions. The traditional view has long been based on the myth that the female spider always kills and eats the male after mating, and that courtship has the effect of postponing the slaughter which, if immediate, would leave the female unfertilized. This opinion neglects the fact that the killing of the male has usually been recorded in cages from which escape, such as would occur in nature, is impossible. It also neglects the widespread occurrence of comparable courtship throughout almost the whole of the animal kingdom, including many animals among which cannibalism is unknown.

In general terms it may be said that all courtship consists of a series of instinctive actions, the result of which is to bring both sexes to the degree of physical stimulation necessary for mating.

In different species of spiders the mating process is almost as variable as the courtship. The male may climb upon or under the female, he may be facing the same way or the opposite way, he may insert into the epigyne both palpi together, or successively, and he may insert each palp once or many times. The two spiders may be associated for a minute or for half an hour.

It is when the mating is over that the peculiar nature of the male spider becomes obvious. The search, possibly involving starvation, the courtship and the mating have been three successively exhausting operations. In fact, many a male arrives at the web of the female so fatigued that he is unable to perform the courtship efficiently; others have been known to die in the act of mating. Mating over, the male has no further biological function and no reason for survival. If he is slow to move away, or if the female is hungry, the death and consumption of the male is to be expected. But the "insurance policy" theory of courtship, picturing the male as precariously poised between terror and desire, is an exaggerated picture of the whole process.

In the female the spermatozoa are stored in spermathecae that communicate with the oviduct or the epigyne and the eggs are fertilized as they are laid. They are small spheres, always contained in a silk cocoon. Cocoons differ a great deal in size, colour, subsequent treatment and the number of eggs they contain. In general, the female spider spins a silk sheet, lays the eggs upon it and spins a second sheet over them. Manipulation of this between the legs, while the spinnerets overspin it with threads, makes a rounded or bun-shaped object, but sometimes, as in the familiar cross-spider, a thick layer of coloured threads surrounds the bag of eggs, and is covered over before the cocoon is fastened to a tree or a fence. The cocoons of some spiders are hung among leaves and a silk nursery is constructed round them; others are carefully covered with mud or with bits of grit; many are attached to the underside of the loose bark of a tree or of a stone or a piece of slate. By far the greater number of cocoons are abandoned altogether and the female takes no further notice of them. The exceptions to this are of some interest.

There are several common species of spiders that carry their cocoons with them, either grasped by the chelicerae or held by the legs, but among the most interesting are all the species of wolf-spiders of the family Lycosidae, which attach their cocoons to their spinnerets.

These spiders appear to show intense maternal care for their cocoons, for they will struggle fiercely to retain them if an attempt is made to remove them. If a cocoon is forcibly removed, the spider seems to be dazed or stupified: she will at once replace it if she touches it, but she is equally ready to carry away any other cocoon or any small object sufficiently like it, such as a pith ball or a sphere of cotton-wool or blotting-paper. Wolf-spiders in nature have been seen carrying small shells.

This fact, combined with the observation that no male spiders and no immature spiders have ever been known to show an inclination to carry anything, indicates that here is an example of a purely feminine instinct. There follows at once the question, How long will a spider "remember" her cocoon and re-attach it when it is returned to her?

The early experiments gave puzzling and inconsistent results: spiders were found to refuse to carry their restored cocoons in a couple of hours, others accepted them after three days. The truth seems to be that the spider's reaction to the cocoon is governed by the state of her ovaries. If a cocoon has been carried for so long that hatching is near, the ovaries are enlarged with well-developed eggs that will soon form the next cocoonful. In these circumstances "memory" is short. But if the lost cocoon is a new one and the ovaries have scarcely begun to prepare the next clutch of eggs, then the carrying instinct is stronger and the cocoon is accepted after a longer interval.

Wolf-spiders, like scorpions, carry their young ones on their backs, but show them very little affection beyond a restraint from eating them. The supreme example of maternal care among spiders is found in one or two species of the genus Theridion, where the mother actually feeds the young ones. They approach her mouth and apply their own mouths to hers, sucking in a fluid which she has secreted. "Spiders' milk" may sound like an impossibility; it is in fact only an example of the incredible surprises that the study of spiders has to offer.

6   *The Spider's Web*

NOTHING in the life of the spider is more characteristic than its web, nor is there in the animal kingdom any better example of the product of instinctive behaviour. Hence any account of the biology of spiders must include a discussion of their webs.

Clearly the making of silk must have preceded the spinning of webs, and equally clearly the various forms of silk glands described in Chapter 3 are the outcome of long ages of evolution. Silk, because of its unusual physical properties, is useful to the spider. In consequence its production was favoured and its uses were multiplied, until it became an essential on which the survival of the spider entirely depended.

Spider silk consists almost wholly of the protein known as fibroin, which is also one of the constituents of silkworm silk. It has a specific gravity of 1·28, an extensibility of about 30 per cent., and a breaking stress greater than that of steel. There are slight differences between the silks secreted by different species of spider, and also between the silks secreted by different glands in the same spider. The really important physical property of silk is its coagulation. In the lumen of a gland and in the duct from it, silk is a viscous fluid. When it is drawn from the spinnerets, either by the wind or by the movement of the spider away from the spot which the spinnerets have touched, it solidifies as a result of the tension developed, which brings about a reorientation of the long chain-like molecules, setting them in the direction of the axis of the thread.

This results in a coagulation which is not a hardening due either to evaporation or oxidation.

To describe how the first spiders made the first webs is as difficult as describing how the first bees made the first honeycombs. In such circumstances, zoologists are compelled to rely on speculation. The nature of silk makes it probable that at its first appearance it took the form of a stream of hardening material exuded by the spider as it moved. Support for this hypothesis comes from the fact that nearly every spider leaves behind it a "drag-line", a double thread of silk fixed at intervals to the ground.

One idea of the origin of webs is based on the above assumption. If the early spider found protection for itself in a chance shelter from which it was in the habit of darting out to seize passing victims, its home would quickly become the centre of a number of radiating threads. The consequence, that insects would touch these threads and so inform the lurking spider of their arrival, is acceptable, and suggests the growth of a web consisting of a silk-lined crevice with a bell-mouth fringe of diverging threads. Many webs of this kind exist (Fig. 29).

Other suggestions have been put forward. Some zoologists believe that the first use of silk was to cover the eggs, others that it was valuable because a drop of semen could be placed on it by the male before being picked up by the palpi. These ideas do not exclude each other; all may have played their parts.

It is evident that the early spiders had hit upon a successful mode of life. They flourished and they spread into different types of environment. While some retained the ancestral insidiatorial habits, others climbed rock faces or tree trunks, some ascended the stems and leaves of small plants, some took to running and some to leaping, some went to the neighbourhood of water or even to the sea, some dug or burrowed into the earth. This account of exploratory activity is not peculiar to spiders; the sentences just written might equally well have been written about mammals or mites or some other group of successful animals. The phenomenon is generally described as adaptive radiation and is accepted as a useful concept by all zoologists. It is extremely helpful in the scientific study of spiders' webs.

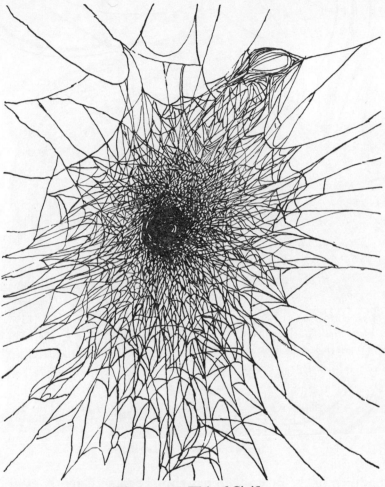

Figure 29. Web of Ciniflo.

Spiders, then, radiated into different environments, and wherever they went they took their silk and their drag-line habit with them. Hence we may look upon the various types of web not as evolving from a single origin but as a number of different consequences resulting from different modes of life in different circumstances and different patterns of innate behaviour.

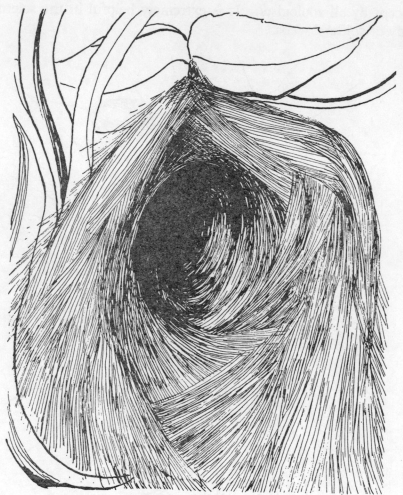

Figure 30. Web of Tegenaria.

The form of the proto-web has thus been sufficiently established and it is clear that its effectiveness is increased by an enlarging of the bell-mouth on the surrounding rock face. Those spiders that climbed into the undergrowth continued to make themselves silk tubes in which to shelter, and they produced the lower lip of the tube horizontally among the stems and leaves. The web was thus a tube-and-sheet construction, and the sheet was often supported by a number of guy-ropes or scaffold-lines above it (Fig. 30).

Flying insects strike this aerial portion and tumble down on to the sheet. This type of web is the basis of the common cobweb, spun by house-spiders in sheds and garages and neglected rooms. Sometimes the sheet becomes relatively enormous, well worthy of the very large spider that it has to support.

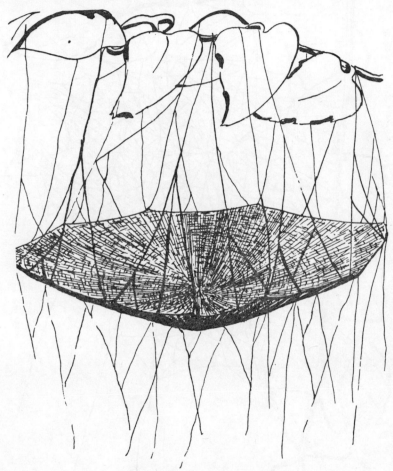

Figure 31. Web of Linyphia.

Two other common types of web might be described as derived from this. The very numerous webs that are to be found in every bush and hedge, but which are usually noticed only when dew or frost has made them conspicuous, may be called hammock-webs.

They may be likened to the sheet of the cobweb, with the valuable superstructure of criss-cross threads above it, but without the tube.   The spider hangs upside down below the sheet and usually bites the insects through the silk (Fig. 31).

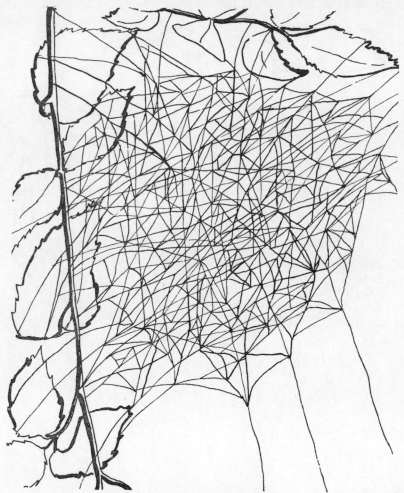

Figure 32.   Web of Theridion.

The second derivative is a web that consists only of the irregular crossing threads without a sheet below them.   The spider lives among them, usually hidden beneath a curled leaf (Fig. 32).

Finally the orb-web of the garden spider is too well known to need description; it is also by far the most puzzling. It is almost impossible to determine how the web originated; it is possible to watch it being made and to note the more or less constant order in which the stages follow each other, but it is very difficult to decide exactly what guides the spider through the process and causes it to make so symmetrical, so perfect, so efficient and so beautiful an object.

Although the complete story of the orb-web remains one of the mysteries of invertebrate biology, the steps that produce it may be briefly outlined. First a horizontal thread, the "bridge-line" is fixed between two convenient spots, and then duplicated by a second thread below it. A third thread is attached to the middle of this and the spider drops on it, pulling down the second thread to form a Y. This is called the fork and its appearance is noted in the making of nearly every orb-web. It marks the limits of the area which the web is to occupy, round which area a thread is now placed, forming a polygonal spinning field (Fig. 33).

Within this field the radii are next spun, being placed alternately first on one side of the centre, then on the other. These radii act first as supports for five or six turns of a rather widely-spaced spiral, which acts as a temporary scaffolding. This provides foothold for the spider during the last stage, the spinning of many turns of a spiral of viscid thread, on which countless tiny drops of gummy secretion, produced by glands in the opisthosoma, known as aggregate glands, are formed. These make escape far more difficult for the captured flies.

The finished orb-web is a structure of symmetry and great beauty and may claim to be among the supreme achievements of instinctive actions. The forces that guide and direct the spider during the long process are imperfectly understood, but there is little doubt that responses to the tensions of the different threads by the spider's delicate muscular sense are partly responsible.

It appears, however, that the operation is mechanically determined and is wholly instinctive in nature. One of the features of a lengthy instinctive process is the impossibility of reversing or repeating any part of it. Thus it has been observed that if a spider

C

is interrupted during the laying down of the spiral thread, and if the part of the spiral already in position is removed, the spider, returning when all is quiet, resumes operations at the point at which it broke off. It adds half a spiral and sits to await results at the centre of half a web.

Figure 33. Stages in the spinning of an orb-web.

Whatever be the form of a web and whatever its origin and development may have been, its operations are the same. It enables the spider to catch its food because it is shaken by the struggles which direct the waiting spider to the victim.

The directing effect is to be noted. It is, in fact, a vibrotaxis to which it is hard to find a parallel among any other animals. It is a perfect example of a telotaxis and was first described in 1915 by Barrows. He used an electrically maintained oscillator to shake a web at various places and photographed web and responding spider by timed flashlight. The pictures showed very clearly how the spider turned itself towards the centre of the disturbance, they showed which threads were vibrating most vigorously, and also how the spider moved across the wave-fronts of the vibrations towards the point of origin.

Further experiment has emphasized the fact that in spiders there is a delicately responsive muscular sense, which, combined with the purely tactile sensitiveness of the setae gives unique and unexpected power. This enables a spider to distinguish differences in tension in the threads of its web. If a garden spider while spinning its spiral thread treads on a radius which is less taut than the rest, it usually turns round and spins the next portion of the spiral in the opposite direction until, perhaps, the same thing recurs.

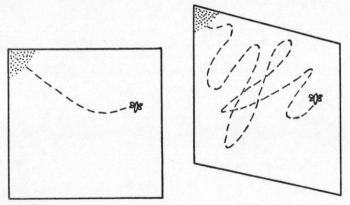

Figure 34. Return of a spider to its retreat, in normal and distorted webs.

If a lifeless object such as a small leaf, a piece of grass, or a little feather is thrown or blown into the web, the shock of its arrival arouses the spider, but because the object does not struggle the spider does not immediately rush to it. With its first legs it jerks gently on a couple of radii, as if testing their tensions, and if these seem to be normal, it turns enough to enable it to test neighbouring radii. Soon it will have pulled on a radius loaded with the object, and now it will cross the web to the intruder, touch it, and probably cut it free and throw it away.

By far the most astonishing example of this muscular sense is shown by the spiders that spin the sheet-and-tube webs of the familiar house spiders. It was shown by Holzapfel that after one of these spiders has seized its victim on the sheet of the web, the return to its corner is directed by the tensions of the threads. She showed that if these tensions were altered by slight distortion of the box containing the web, the returning spider lost its way and only reached its goal by a very devious path (Fig. 34). This peculiar behaviour, more than any other type of action, marks spiders as unique among the animals of the world.

7 _Other Arachnida_

SPIDERS, it was said in the first chapter of this book, form one of the eleven orders of living Arachnida, and six of these orders were named because they include arachnids that are familiar or widely distributed or of special interest. An account of spiders, such as has been given in the foregoing pages, is more valuable if it is supplemented by some description of spiders' allies. The names of these five orders of the Arachnida are:

Scorpiones	scorpions
Pseudoscorpiones	false-scorpions
Opiliones	harvestmen
Solifugae	wind-scorpions
Acari	mites and ticks.

Scorpions

Scorpions are certainly the most familiar of these orders, and, apart from their human and historical interest, they are of some biological importance, since they are always regarded as the most primitive order of the land-dwelling arachnids. There is good evidence that at least some genera of the earliest scorpions actually lived in the water, while others were beginning to leave it and become the first inhabitants of dry land.

In its general appearance a scorpion (Fig. 35) is very different from a spider. It possesses, first, a pair of very large pedipalpi, which are more like the "claws" of a lobster than the leg-like palpi of a spider, and which provide the scorpion with very effective means of seizing and holding its prey.

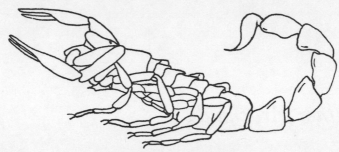

Figure 35. A scorpion.

Scorpions do not possess the narrow pedicel which in spiders unites prosoma and opisthosoma. The latter is characteristic. It

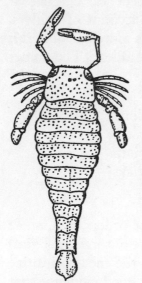

Figure 36. A Eury-pterid.

is obviously segmented from end to end, and it is divisible into a mesosoma of seven somites, followed by a narrower five-somite metasoma, colloquially called the "tail". The tail ends in a sting, supplied from a poison-gland contained in the telson. Clearly, both the size of the pedipalpi and the existence of a unique venom-system are specializations rather than primitive features. The description of scorpions as primitive is largely based on a general resemblance to the extinct Eurypterida (Fig. 36), a group which is often regarded as the ancestors of the scorpions. The evidence supporting this belief does not convince every zoologist; but one of the most interesting details concerns the respiratory organs. Eurypterids, as befits aquatic creatures, had gills or branchiae, five pairs of them underneath the mesosomatic sternites. Scorpions have four pairs of lung-books on the third to the sixth somites. These are hollows or invaginations of the exoskeleton, containing a number of blood-filled plates, and may not inaccurately be regarded as eurypterid gills adapted for use in air.

In addition to these characteristics, all scorpions carry a pair of unique organs of uncertain function. These are the pectines, so called because they resemble combs, found on the lower surface of the opisthosoma in front of the first pair of lung-books. They are probably derived from the first pair of gills of the eurypterid ancestors, and their value to the scorpion has long puzzled zoologists. They carry setae and so probably act as sense-organs of a tactile nature; there is also evidence that they respond to chemical stimuli and inform the scorpion of the nature of the ground over which it is walking and of the presence of food thereon. It is also possible that they react to vibrations of the ground and to vibrations of the air, but whatever they do a scorpion from which they have been removed does not seem to be handicapped.

All these specializations remind us that no animal customarily and correctly described as primitive is completely primitive in every respect. There are always some special adaptations, which probably play a vital part in survival by compensating for simplicity elsewhere.

The sting in the scorpion's telson is one example of such a specialization. The metasoma or tail of a scorpion is very mobile and at the threat of danger is arched over the animal's back, ready to strike forwards at an aggressor. The poison, like that of the spider, is quickly fatal to the scorpion's normal prey. Its effect on man is variable, some species being much more dangerous and painful than others; but the general position is that casualties from scorpion-stings are serious and frequent enough to have inspired a good deal of research and the production of an effective antitoxin.

Scorpions are confined to hot or to very hot regions of the world and are among the outstanding arachnids of the deserts. They are protected against excessive loss of moisture by a layer of wax in the cuticle, and when they become uncomfortably hot they have a curious habit of straightening their legs and raising themselves as if on stilts. This helps to control their body temperatures.

A very elaborate courtship is undertaken by the mature animals; the male grasps the female with his chelicerae and, with tails arched, they move about together for several minutes. A time comes when the male, touching the ground with his pectines, finds that it is smooth enough for his purpose. This smoothness has been proved to be an essential. He then produces a spermatophore.

A spermatophore is a structure that is not found among spiders, where the sperm-web takes its place. It is secreted from the body of the male and quickly hardens into a pillar, of peculiar and characteristic shape (Fig. 37). Upon it a drop of semen is placed and finally the male scorpion leads the female to a position in which the spermatophore enters her body, carrying the spermatozoa with it. This method of insemination is found among false-scorpions and some other Arachnida, and the precision and positioning which it demands is the probable origin of "courtship" in these animals.

Figure 37. Spermatophore of a scorpion.

One of the special features of the life of scorpions is that the young ones are born alive, instead of hatching from eggs. This is the only case of viviparity among the Arachnida. Young scorpions spend the first few days of their lives on their mother's back, a form of maternal care which has been mentioned earlier as occurring among wolf-spiders. The number born to one female in a year is only about fifty, and the survival of the race with so low a reproductive capacity is to be attributed partly to this habit and partly to the absence of natural enemies in the regions that scorpions normally occupy.

False-scorpions

These arachnids owe their popular name to their large pedipalpi

(Fig. 38) which are relatively even longer than those of scorpions. In most other ways they are very different. Whereas scorpions are, in general, the largest of the Arachnida, pseudoscorpions are among the smallest, with few species more than 5 mm. long. The prosoma is covered, like that of a scorpion, with an unsegmented carapace, bearing two or four eyes; the abdomen has neither tail nor telson. It is a smooth oval shape and is fully segmented, with eleven distinct tergites. The twelfth tergite is very small and, united to the twelfth sternite, forms a terminal ring round the anus.

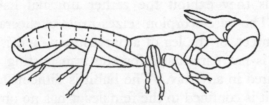

Figure 38. A false-scorpion.

Unlike scorpions, pseudoscorpions are ubiquitous and twenty-four species occur in Britain. They live under fallen leaves and under the bark of trees; some live among sand or stones, some in old bird's nests and some with ants. A few live near the sea and a few sometimes enter our houses. The sifting of a handful of fallen leaves in a wood is almost sure to yield one or two specimens.

They are recognizable at once. As soon as they have recovered from the shock of falling they spread out their great pedipalpi and walk with sedate deliberation, their palpi acting as sense organs as do the antennae of an insect. If they touch anything disturbing, they draw in their palpi and rush backwards much more rapidly than they have been going forwards.

Other features distinguish them from all other orders of arachnids. They have silk glands in the small chelicerae in front of their mouths, and they use their silk to make egg cocoons and for building. Before the eggs are laid the false-scorpion makes around itself a small circle of pieces of grit. Upon these it places more grit, holding the pieces in position by sweeping silk over them, and continuing in this way

c*

until it has enclosed itself completely. Here the eggs are laid. After they have hatched the young are fed by the mother, to whose genital orifice they are at first attached by a short "beak". Changes in the ovaries produce a secretion, "uterine milk", which the young false-scorpions imbibe.

There are venom glands in the chelicerae, opening at small teeth on one or on both of the pincers. False-scorpions are purely carnivorous, and with a bite from their chelicerae kill instantane-ously insects and spiders as large as themselves. They consume their prey entirely, leaving no scraps.

At intervals they exhibit the rather unusual habit known as "phoresy". The false-scorpion seizes in its chelicerae the leg of a fly or other insect, or the leg of a harvestman, and is carried away by it. This is not parasitism, for the transporting animal is not bitten or injured in any way. The habit is difficult to understand, for although it is confined to the females it has no obvious correla-tion with breeding. A possible explanation is that it is a reaction to hunger, occurring when or where food is scarce.

The courtship of false-scorpions resembles that of the true scorpions. The partners grasp each other by their chelicerae, move to and fro, backwards and forwards in concert for some time, until the male deposits a spermatophore on the ground and leads the female over it.

Pseudoscorpions are among the most fascinating of small animals, deserving more attention than they get, and there is as yet much to be learnt about them. Apart from this they may be described zoologically as the most representative order of the class Arachnida, closely resembling, in their typical form, what an "average arachnid" ought to be. For example, they are not large, they are widespread, fairly rich in number of species, carnivorous and nocturnal. They have simple eyes, so ineffective that they are largely superseded by tactile setae, broad waists, segmented bodies, normal legs and other appendages. This is a combination of characteristics which ought to have been recognized by zoologists and proclaimed by them as making false-scorpions the most suitable order to stand as a type or representative of the class Arachnida.

Opiliones

The harvestmen (Fig. 39), which form this order, are more familiar than false-scorpions; they are much larger and are often seen in woods and fields, especially in the autumn, running rather clumsily but quite quickly, on their very long legs. A score of species are known in Britain and about two thousand in the world, but the British species do not include the harvestmen with fantastic bodies, covered with spines and spikes and teeth, that occur elsewhere.

Figure 39.   A harvestman.

The body of a harvestman is usually a regular oval in shape, with no more than a deep groove marking the boundary between pro-soma and opisthosoma. The carapace covering the former bears not far behind its fore-edge an ocularium or eye-turret, on which are two eyes, placed back to back and staring sideways. Segmentation of the opisthosoma is obvious in some species and more obscure in others. The number of somites is ten, unusually arranged. The foremost sternites constitute a plate or genital operculum covering the orifice of the sex-organs, and this has pulled the other sternites forwards, so that the anus is not terminal but underneath, and any one sternite lies in front of a perpendicular line from its corresponding tergite (Fig. 40).

The chelicerae are three-jointed appendages in the form of small claws and the pedipalpi six-jointed and leg-like. The legs, as already mentioned, are usually long and in some species very long, perhaps twenty or more times as long as the body. The last segment, the tarsus, is divided into sub-segments of which there may be only a few or as many as a hundred. The legs are therefore conspicuous, mobile and sensitive organs and much of a harvest-man's life depends on them. The second pair are often the longest and to some extent act like the antennae of an insect. The loss of a second leg is a more serious handicap to the harvestman than the loss of one of the others.

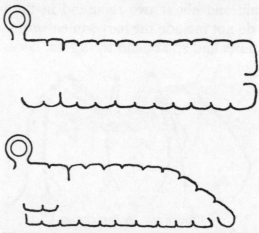

Figure 40. Arrangement of tergites and ster-nites in a primitive arachnid and in a harvest-man (below).

In view of this it is a surprise to find that a harvestman's legs are easily shed by the process of autotomy described in Chapter 4, and that when the animal moults the lost leg is not regenerated. The coxa remains among the others but smaller than any of them, and the harvestman spends the rest of its life with fewer legs. In fact, towards the end of the year harvestmen with all eight legs are scarcely more plentiful than those with seven or six. The failure to regenerate lost legs is remarkable, and harvestmen seem to be the only arachnids in which the loss of a leg is permanent.

Harvestmen have, further, a peculiar method of protecting themselves. In the prosoma, at the level of the second pair of legs, there is a pair of odoriferous glands, usually visible through the carapace and looking like a second pair of eyes. Above each gland there is a small aperture and when the harvestman is irritated, threatened or otherwise stimulated the glands secrete a noisome vapour. In extreme cases the secretion can be seen as a drop of liquid or as a fine spray. It is not particularly obvious to human noses, nor is it noticeably unpleasant.

Harvestmen have never been described as undertaking any form of courtship. Their behaviour in this respect is in sharp contrast to that of all other Arachnida, for the male possesses an intromittent organ (Fig. 41), in direct connexion with the testes and vas deferentia, which is thrust beneath the female operculum. There is seldom any risk that either partner will attack the other; but more significant is the fact that there is no preliminary courtship where there is no spermatophore.

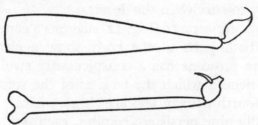

Figure 41. Penis of *Oligolophus tridens*, above, and *O. agrestis*, below.

The female has an expansible oviduct (Fig. 41) which she pushes into damp soil to lay the eggs a few millimetres underground. The tiny harvestmen which hatch from them are seemingly feeble little creatures, not at all easy to rear in the laboratory.

Harvestmen are not as particular about their food as are spiders or false-scorpions. They can be kept alive and in health on a diet of bread and fat, for their food does not need to be alive before they will eat it. In natural circumstances they have been recorded as taking a wide variety of substances, of which perhaps the most surprising is fruit juice. They can often be seen in the garden sucking up the liquid from the wounds in fallen pears or apples. At all times they drink quantities of water. They cannot withstand either hunger or thirst as long as spiders can, and if water is not available they become stiff and torpid. Then, given the opportunity, they will drink greedily and in a very few minutes will regain their usual activity.

Clearly, harvestmen form an individualistic order, and if they had any economic importance, or if they advertised themselves with anything as conspicuous as a spider's web they would successfully challenge spiders as the most popular type of arachnid.

Solifugae

The wind-scorpions (or sun-spiders or camel-spiders) are, like scorpions proper, arachnids of moderate size, reaching a body-length of six or seven centimetres. They were recognized by the ancient writers and mentioned by Pliny, but in popular esteem they have always been overshadowed by scorpions, with whom they share an ability to survive in the desert.

Their outward appearance (Fig. 42) suggests a generally primitive arachnid, for both parts of the body show a clearly segmental structure. The prosoma has a conspicuously swollen "head" or propeltidium, behind which the tergites of the somites that carry the third and fourth pairs of legs are clearly visible. The opisthosoma has usually nine persistent somites, each one with its tergite and sternite, very much as is seen in the false-scorpions.

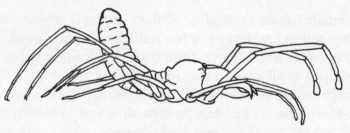

Figure 42. A solifuge.

The most noticeable of the special characteristics is the great size of the forwardly-directed chelicerae, which make the Solifugae, for their size, the most formidably armed animals in the world. In all species they are very powerful: they contain no venom but rely for their destructiveness on muscular strength alone.

The pedipalpi are leg-like limbs of six segments. The last segment or tarsus does not end in a claw but in a peculiar sucker, used by the animal in climbing, in picking up food, in drinking and as a buffer in combat. The legs of Solifugae are also unusual. The legs of the first pair are longer and thinner than the others; they are not used in walking, but are held stretched forward, acting like the second pair of legs in the harvestmen, as sense-organs. The legs of the fourth pair carry on their first two segments mysterious objects called racket-organs or malleoli. Their function has not been satisfactorily described, and they help to emphasize the highly characteristic nature of the order of Solifugae.

The whole of the body of a solifuge is covered with setae which give the animal a very "hairy" appearance. Some of these setae are as much as 2 cm. long and so sensitive that the lightest touch on the tip of one seta provokes an immediate response.

Solifugae are nocturnal and carnivorous, spending the day in a burrow which they dig with their chelicerae, and searching for food in the evenings. They eat insects, spiders, scorpions and lizards, and are unusually voracious, inclined to continue feeding until they are so bloated that they can scarcely move. Their prey is held transversely between the forceps of the chelicerae and chewed with such vigour that a solifuge eating a beetle can be heard at a distance of several yards.

Solifugae are pugnacious creatures. They fight ferociously with scorpions, centipedes and with each other. Swiftness and strength in battle take the place of venom and subtlety, and contests may be prolonged and spectacular. Only seldom, and more or less by accident, do Solifugae bite human beings.

A further characteristic of these arachnids is their speed. In sharp contrast to the slow-moving scorpions of their neighbourhood, they rush about with great rapidity, often looking like moving balls of hair; and since some species occasionally enter tents or houses they have popularly inspired more fear or respect than they deserve.

The mating habits of Solifugae are different from those in other orders. The only form of courtship which the male undertakes is a gentle stroking of the female with his pedipalpi and forelegs. This reduces her to an impassive state, as if anaesthetized, whereupon the male picks her up in his chelicerae and lays her on her side. Raising his body, he ejects a mass of spermatozoa upon the ground; picks it up with his chelicerae and forces it into the vagina. He closes the operculum, holding the edges together for a few moments, and then departs.

It is probable that there is more to be discovered about the Solifugae than about any of the other orders mentioned in this chapter.

Mites

Mites and ticks are united in a rather heterogeneous order which in a number of ways stands apart from the rest of the class. Many of them lead lives which make them a nuisance and a source of expense; in other words they are often parasites or pests, a fact which gives them an economic importance and is reflected in so many distinctive features that some taxonomists have placed them in a separate sub-class, or even in a class by themselves. As an example of a purely biological characteristic, the fact that many mites hatch as larvae with only six legs may be mentioned.

The present custom is to divide mites into six sub-orders:

Notostigmata	Parasitiformes	Sarcoptiformes
Holothyroidea	Trombidiformes	Tetrapodili.

The first two of these groups contain rare and primitive species, which almost wholly retain the original segmentation of the body. In each of the other four there are species which are well known for different reasons.

Ticks, the largest and most familiar of the Acari, belong to the third sub-order, the Parasitiformes. One of the most familiar is the sheep-tick, *Ixodes ricinus* (Fig. 43), a common pest of sheep and one which often attaches itself to our dogs. A serious parasite of poultry is *Argas persicus*, while a very well-known tick, *Ornithodorus moubata*, attacks man and is the cause of relapsing fever in Africa.

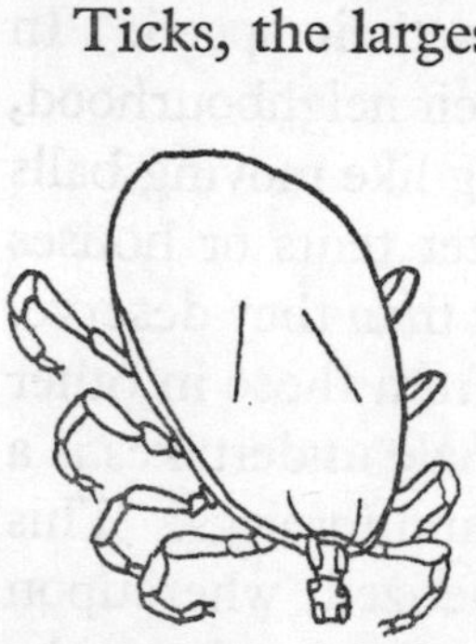

Figure 43. A tick.

In the Trombidiformes is included one of the smallest of all mites, the species *Acarapis woodi*. This is only a fraction of a millimetre in length and lives

inside the tracheal tubes of the honey-bee. It is the cause of suffo-
cation known as Isle of Wight disease. In the same sub-order are
the equally minute skin parasites of the genus Demodex, extremely
common in the hair follicles of man and one of the causes of
mange in dogs; also the familiar "red-spiders", Tetranychus, and
the very irritating "harvest-bugs", responsible for scrub-typhus.

The Sarcoptiformes are best represented by *Sarcoptes scabiei*, the
itch-mite, which burrows and lays eggs in the human skin; and
the most notorious of the Tetrapodili is *Eriophyes ribis*, the parasite
that causes "big-bud" in currants.

It is clear that mites deserve all the attention that economic
zoologists can give them. They rival insects in their anti-social
activities, and, unlike insects, they do not seem to include any
species that are helpful to man.

Xiphosura

It may be helpful to end this chapter with a short statement about
the well-known king-crab, often called Limulus.

In 1881 E. Ray Lankester published a paper in which he described
Limulus as an arachnid living in the sea and showing relationships
on one hand to the extinct Eurypterida and on the other to living
scorpions. His conclusions were fully discussed before their
acceptance was secured.

The king-crab has an unusual appearance. Its prosoma is shaped
like a horse shoe with sloping sides; the posterior margin has a three-
sided re-entrant into which fits the hexagonal opisthosoma. The
body can be resolved into fifteen somites, and their appendages
follow the usual plan. The chelicerae are small pincer-like organs
of three segments. The second pair of appendages cannot properly
be called pedipalps, for they differ in no essential from the four
pairs that follow and Limulus may be described as having five pairs
of legs. A most interesting feature is the position of the mouth,
which lies between the coxae of the legs, all of which surround it
and have gnathobases assisting in mastication. Thus the mouth
of Limulus lies further back than in any other group of arachnids
except the extinct Stethostomata mentioned in the next chapter.

Behind the mouth there lies a seventh pair of appendages, the chilaria, small round plates joined together at the base. Their function is doubtful.

One of the chief characteristics of Limulus is the possession of six pairs of mesosomatic appendages, in the form of flat, semi-circular plates. The first is known as the genital operculum, since it lies upon the genital orifice. The five that follow carry respiratory organs in the form of gill-books, and the close structural resemblance between these and the lung-books of scorpions is one of the closest resemblances between the two orders.

The metasoma is reduced to a vestige composed of three somites which can be recognized only in the embryo. Finally, the body ends with a long and conspicuous telson in the form of a spine. This is used by the king-crab to right itself if it falls on its back, and it is also thrust into the sand when the animal moves forwards.

Recent opinion has separated the Eurypterida, Limulus and a few other forms from the essentially terrestrial Arachnida and has grouped them in a class known as the Merostomata. The extinct members of the Merostomata are of great value in deducing the evolution of the Arachnida and determining their relationships.

8 *Classification*

IN the first chapter of this book it was stated that the sub-phylum of the Arthropoda known as the Chelicerata is divisible into a marine class, the Merostomata, which includes the extinct Eurypterida and the living king-crabs, Limulus and its allies, and a terrestrial class, the Arachnida, with sixteen orders, of which the spiders form the largest.

A satisfactory arrangement of these orders, following and illustrating their evolutionary progress from the most primitive to the most specialized, presents a problem which is not unknown in other classes of animals and is very well exemplified by the Arachnida. When each order consists of species which have added to a fundamental similarity of structure different specializations, any evolutionary series must depend on an evaluation of these acquisitions. Hence there arise such questions as—Which characteristic is the more primitive, the possession of silk-glands in the opisthosoma or of poison-glands in the chelicerae? Or the presence or absence of pincers on the pedipalpi? Or the existence of two or three claws on the legs?

Even if it be granted that all these questions, and twice as many more like them, can be answered, there follow more difficult decisions as to the relative significance of different permutations and combinations of the alternatives involved. These are problems of advanced arachnology, which call for discussion and agreement before zoologists can decide on a generally acceptable method of classifying the group.

In one of the most recently proposed systems, the Arachnida are divided into four sub-classes which are called

Latigastra   Soluta

Stethostomata   Caulogastra

These are unfamiliar words. They were given to groups of arachnid orders by Professor Alexander Petrunkevitch in 1949 in his efforts to produce an alternative to a simple list of orders with no steps or stages between order and class, an alternative scheme which would follow, or at least suggest, possible trends in evolution.

The sub-class **Latigastra** is characterized by a broad junction between prosoma and opisthosoma, fusion being complete across the whole width of the body. The first opisthosomatic somite tends to shorten, and has disappeared altogether from some orders. The carapace is always unsegmented. There is a tendency towards a reduction of the posterior somites, which, like the first, become shorter. This sub-class includes the orders:

Scorpiones   scorpions

Pseudoscorpiones   false-scorpions

Opiliones   harvestmen

Acari   mites

Architarbi

The first four of these were shortly described in the last chapter.

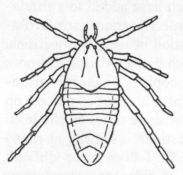

Figure 44.   Architarbus.

The Architarbi (Fig. 44) occur only in the Carboniferous strata. They show a peculiar shortening of several of the anterior somites of the opisthosoma, and possess an elongated sternum of three sternites. About twenty-five species have been found.

The **Stethostomata** are all extinct, Carboniferous, forms. In most Arachnida the chelicerae are placed higher than the pedipalpi and legs; in this sub-class they are on the same level and are wedged in between the coxae of the pedipalpi so that the mouth has perforce moved backwards, and lies between the coxae of the first legs. There are two orders,

Haptopoda (Fig. 45) with but a single species, and Anthracomarti, with about twenty.

The **Soluta** contain the order Trigonotarbi (Fig. 46) only, characterized by a junction between the two halves of the body which covers the middle third of the width of the somites. There are from eight to eleven opisthosomatic somites; in other respects these arachnids tend to resemble spiders. Nearly forty species have been described, all from the Carboniferous rocks.

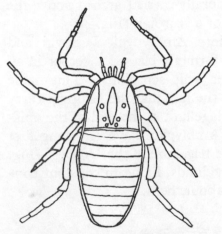
Figure 45. A haptopod.

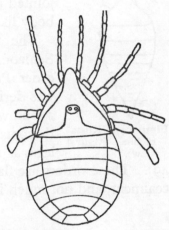
Figure 46. Trigonotarbus.

The **Caulogastra** contain all those orders in which a narrow pedicel unites the two parts of the body, a pedicel derived from a somite that has been reduced in diameter rather than in length. The carapace retains segmentation in some orders, notably in the Solifugae. There is a tendency towards a reduction of the posterior somites of the opisthosoma, which may become narrowed to form a tail-like pygidium, as in the order Schizomide, or may nearly vanish, leaving only a vestige like the colulus in spiders. The Latigastra and the Caulogastra represent two different and probably parallel paths of evolution.

The Caulogastra are composed of eight orders:

Kustarachnae	Uropygi	Solifugae
Palpigradi	Schizomida	Ricinulei
Amblypygi	Araneida	

The Kustarachnae are extinct forms, known only from the Carboniferous, as a single genus, Kustarachne, with three species.

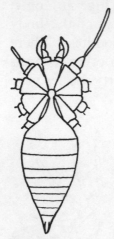

They show the remarkable feature of a complete fusion of the pedipalpal coxae; and the coxae of the legs are large and triangular, radiating from a small sternum (Fig. 47).

The Palpigradi are an order of very small arachnids, in which the opisthosoma carries a long jointed telson, generally carried arched above the body like the tail of a scorpion (Fig. 48).

The three orders Amblypygi, Uropygi and Schizomida were formerly classed together in an order Pedipalpi or whip-scorpions. This name was derived from the fact that the Uropygi carry a long whip-like flagellum at the end of the opis-

Figure 47. Kusta-rachne (ventral view).

thosoma, and the Amblypygi have very long first legs, as thin as the flagellum of the Uropygi (Fig. 49). These orders are flattened arachnids, living in constant concealment, and not much is known about them.

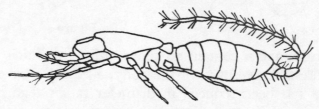

Figure 48. A palpigrade.

The Ricinulei are among the rarest and queerest animals in the world: almost every specimen that has ever been found, either in Central America or Central Africa in 120 years, can be traced and the finding of one is a zoological event. They have extraordinarily thick exoskeletons, a remarkable device by which prosoma and opisthosoma can be locked together, and the male sex organs are in the tarsi of the third legs.

Since spiders are the largest and in every respect the dominant and most important of all the sixteen orders, and since this book is

primarily about them, it is necessary to look briefly at the classification of the Araneida.

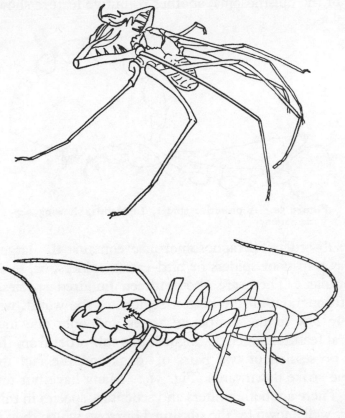

Figure 49.   An amblypyge, above, and a uropyge, below.

With the omission of a few rare forms, the order is divisible into
three sub-orders:

    Liphistiomorphae
    Theraphosomorphae=Mygalomorphae
    Gnaphosomorphae =Araneomorphae

The first of these contains about a dozen species of the family
Liphistiidae. These spiders, which are found only in Malaysia,
China and Japan, are of great interest because they bear on their
opisthosomas a series of plates or tergites, and so retain, to some
extent, external evidence of the originally segmental structure of all

Arachnida (Fig. 50). In addition they have the full complement
of eight spinnerets occupying a position in the middle of the lower
surface of the opisthosoma, another primitive feature shown by no
other spiders.

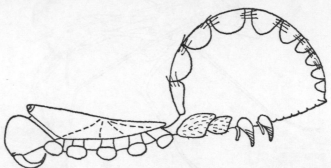

Figure 50. A primitive spider, Liphistius, showing segmentation.

The sub-order Theraphosomorphae contains the large spiders
known as trap-door spiders or bird-eating spiders, or, in America,
as tarantulas. There are about fifteen hundred species, widely
spread throughout all the hottest regions of the world, with com-
paratively few in the temperate zones and only one in Britain.
Structural features which distinguish this sub-order from the others
are the possession of two pairs of lungs and the fact that their
chelicerae strike downwards (Fig. 51). Many have but four spinnerets. There are both hunters and sedentary species in this group,
the latter well known for the silk-lined burrows which they excavate
and close with amazingly inconspicuous trap-doors. Some of these
spiders have a life-span of over twenty years.

The third sub-order, the Gnaphosomorphae, contains about
sixty families and about forty thousand species. They are divisible
artificially into those with a cribellum and those without this organ;
on a behavioural basis into web-spinners and hunters; and naturally
into those with two claws or three claws on each tarsus.

Among the hunting spiders the most representative families are
the wolf-spiders, the Lycosidae, the jumping spiders, the Salticidae,
and the crab-spiders, the Thomisidae. All these are large families,
widely distributed and having many representatives in Britain.

A family related to the Thomisidae and known as the Sparassidae contains the well-known "banana-spider", *Heteropoda venatoria*, that is often imported with bunches of bananas.

Figure 51. Atypus, a mygalomorph spider, showing large chelicerae.

The web-spinners include, first, the cribellate spiders, many of which belong to the family Dictynidae. The rough bluish silk of which their webs are made is often easily recognizable on palings, gateposts and in cellars and out-houses. The form is the early one, a tube with an extended bell-mouth (Fig. 29).

The Theridiidae spin irregular webs, usually in hedges and bushes. The many species of this family are easily identified by the characteristic comb of fairly large setae on the tarsus of each fourth leg. With this comb they draw out sheets of silk from their spinnerets and throw it over captured insects that are struggling in the web. In this way they can overcome victims that are much larger than themselves. The spiders of this family are often brightly coloured, as if to match the leaves and flowers among which they live.

The family Agelenidae includes the house-spiders, the makers of the domestic "cobwebs", and their out-of-door relatives; the so-called Cardinal spider, popularly associated with Hampton Court, where it is said to have frightened Cardinal Wolsey, is one of these; other species of the same genus, Tegenaria, are widespread in houses all over the temperate zone.

The Linyphiidae are among the smallest spiders. They hang upside down below the sheet of a "hammock-web," and are one of

the largest families in cool countries. They illustrate exceedingly
well a principle of the geographical distribution of spiders, the fact
that the largest species live in the hottest regions and the smallest in
the coldest areas. Nearly all the spiders recorded from north of
the Arctic Circle are species less than two millimetres long belonging
to this family.

The Argiopidae are the spinners of the attractive webs known as
orb-webs, geometrical-webs or wheel-webs, and the world-wide
Araneus diadematus, our garden spider, is the most familiar representative. The white cross on its back makes it recognizable at a
glance, and many species of the family have more elaborate and
more beautiful patterns. In tropical countries, spiders of this
family reach a great size and spin webs of considerable strength
spanning an area that may be seven or eight feet across.

Two conclusions may reasonably be drawn from the foregoing
chapters.

As to spiders themselves, it is clear that they owe their biological
success to their exploitation of silk. Then in consequence of the
great number of species endless problems arise for systematists and
the variety of habits of spiders provide equally endless opportunities
for observation by those who are interested in animal behaviour.
In both these ways spiders can challenge or even surpass the
insects.

9 *Laboratory and Field Work*

SPIDERS are good material both for work in the laboratory, which will emphasize the features described in the morphological section at the beginning of this book, and for field work, which will show the zoologist something of how a spider lives, introduce him to the variety of the common species and will probably suggest fresh problems for study.

In the Laboratory

Large spiders, such as the garden spider, *Araneus diadematus*, or the house spider, *Tegenaria atrica*, are easily obtained. They are best killed with chloroform, and if necessary they may be preserved in 70 per cent. alcohol before examination or dissection.

After a thorough scrutiny of the entire animal and a comparison with Figs. 1 and 2, a more detailed study should be made of various parts. A leg, a pedipalp and one of the chelicerae should be removed, not by forceful pulling off, but by cutting the softer membrane where the appendage joins the body with the tip of a small scalpel. Pulling at a limb usually leaves the coxa or the coxa and trochanter attached to the prosoma.

These limbs, separately or together, should be put into 5 per cent. potash and gently boiled. This dissolves all the soft tissues and leaves the chitinous exoskeleton. If the boiling is done in a porcelain evaporating basin there is less chance of bumping, which throws the parts on to the bench, than if a test-tube is used; moreover, the progress of the action is more easily seen against the white background. Three to five minutes boiling is generally sufficient. The parts are then transferred to tap-water to wash away the alkali; they are tough enough to go straight from water to alcohol for dehydration, and are then mounted as microscopical objects in the usual way. They do not need to be stained.

An alternative method, which though somewhat slower, is sometimes helpful, is to clear the object in warm 5 per cent. potash in 70 per cent. alcohol. Delicate organisms remain rigid in the alcohol, and the process of clearing can be more accurately controlled.

Under the microscope all the details mentioned in Chapter 2 can be clearly seen. These include the different types of setae, their mode of insertion in a little crater on the exoskeleton, their regular arrangement on the segments, the form of the tarsal claws and the number of their teeth. The chelicerae should be mounted with the fang opened, thus exposing the teeth on the basal segment.

The examination of a leg can be carried a stage further. If a detached leg is over-boiled in potash, it sheds its hairy coating of setae, and the smooth segments when mounted reveal the puzzling lyriform organs and the chemo-receptive tarsal organ.

The spinnerets should be treated rather differently. If the group is cut off and mounted as a whole they tend to cover each other and prevent close scrutiny. It is better to choose a house-spider, which has particularly long spinnerets, to remove one of them and to mount it separately. The spools and spigots from which the silk issues can then be clearly seen.

Other external features from which slides should be made are the cribellum and the epigyne. A small area of the exoskeleton surrounding the organ is cut out, the fragment treated with warm potash to clean it, and then mounted as before. All the above organs are mentioned in Chapter 2.

The male organs in the palpi require and deserve rather different treatment. Both palpi are needed. One of them should be removed from its coxa, dehydrated, cleared and mounted without further treatment. This shows the form of the palpal organ as it appears when at rest and as the collector sees it when he is determining the identity of a species. The other palp is given the familiar treatment of three minutes' boiling in potash, and this process has the effect of fully expanding all parts of the sex-organ. When this is washed and mounted its complexity can be seen and appreciated (Fig. 6). If the operation is repeated with a spider of a different family the range of variation in this organ is made obvious, and provides an introduction to one of the chief details in the identification of spiders.

The dissecting of a spider, to reveal at least something of its internal structure, should certainly be attempted. A large house-spider is the best species to choose. It is treated in just the same way as the familiar laboratory cockroach, that is to say it is first embedded in wax. The simplest way to do this is to melt the wax of the dissecting dish over an area about as big as a halfpenny by lightly touching it with the tip of a Bunsen flame. The body of the spider is then dropped into the liquid and legs arranged round it as the wax solidifies.

The smallest scissors, needles and needle-knives are the instruments needed, and it is well to make the cutting-edge of the latter as sharp as possible with hone and strop. Chitin is not soft and scalpel blades are not made of the hardest steel.

The work is made easier if a good lens is supported horizontally over the animal to form a simple dissecting microscope. The procedure is not very different from a dissection of the crayfish, on a smaller scale. The carapace is removed after making a cut all round its edges, and the opisthosoma is opened after a longitudinal incision has been made on each side of the central stripe which marks the position of the heart.

The following organs can now be detected, freed from surrounding tissue, removed, stained and mounted. In the prosoma the most conspicuous object is the large endosternite, a plate of chitin which forms an important part of the endoskeleton and is different from anything in the crayfish or cockroach. The sucking stomach and the curved oesophagus in front of it (Fig. 15) are also easily detected among the masses of muscle that fill most of the inside.

In the abdomen it is easy to find the heart, the ovaries and several different types of silk glands. All these essential parts of a spider's anatomy can be extracted, stained and mounted with no greater skill than has been acquired in the successful removal of an earthworm's ovary or nephridium. The endosternite can be cleaned in very dilute potash and, if necessary, stained with picric acid. The soft tissues can be stained quite satisfactorily by simple methods. They are placed successively in 30 per cent. alcohol, 50 per cent. alcohol, borax carmine, 50 per cent., 70 per cent., 90 per cent., and absolute alcohol, and lastly cleared in clove oil and mounted. Over the years my Sixth Form zoologists have made a number of preparations quite as good as any to be seen in the publications of the experts, and a great deal better than some.

Spiders have been described by Professor Millot as being ideal laboratory animals, capable of leading a normal life in captivity, and useful for a variety of investigations into invertebrate physiology. It is reasonable to know how a spider may be kept in a laboratory, if for no more ambitious a purpose than just to see how it lives. House-spiders of the genus Tegenaria are probably the most satisfactory kind to keep. The cage is an ordinary rectangular box, the lid is a sheet of glass or perspex, and in one corner a folded strip of paper makes a spot that is darker than the rest (Fig. 52). The spider spins the tubular part of its web inside this small shed, and lives in it, with its forefeet always in communication with the sheet of web that fills the rest of the box.

Food is supplied in the form of living flies, for which purpose a hole at one end of the box, closed with a cork, is convenient. Feeding about twice a week is usually sufficient; a spider that is given a fly every day is being overfed.

In such cages as these spiders can be observed preening, catching flies, moulting and mating; and their reactions to scents and sounds can be determined. It may be added that harvestmen and false-scorpions are as easy to keep alive and under observation, as long as their need for water is remembered.

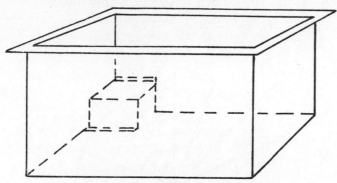

Figure 52. A spider's cage.

In the Field

Spiders are very good subjects for ecologists. The neglect of spiders, so widespread thirty or forty years ago, was no doubt responsible for the delay in the recognition of this side of arachnology: today new ecological studies based on spiders are appearing steadily. A couple of simple illustrative examples may be given.

An important preliminary in ecology is certainty as to the identity of the species under examination; in other words the species most suitable for ecologists to study should be distinctive or easily recognized and named. There are two species that call attention to themselves by spinning orb-webs in which two adjacent sectors have no spiral threads (Fig. 53) and a bare radius runs from the hub to the spider's place of concealment. They are *Zygiella atrica* and *Zygiella x-notata*, species which are similar in general appearance but differ in that the former spins on shrubs and bushes, the latter on walls, sheds and window-frames. Since the fundamental question that an ecologist asks of any animal or plant is Why is it here?, this contrast in choice of environment is an obvious challenge. Experiment showed that *Z. atrica* tended to move into and remain in a moister atmosphere, while *Z. x-notata* moved from a moist atmosphere into a drier one. This tendency was named hygrotropism: today it would be termed hygrotaxis. Its discovery was among the first observations to call attention to the great significance of the moisture of the air in the lives of invertebrates. Much has since been written on this topic.

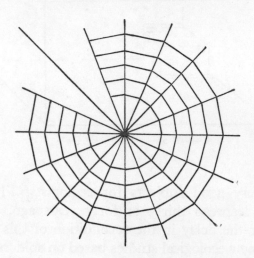

Figure 53. Web of Zygiella (diagramatic).

A second example concerns the wolf-spiders. Easily recognized by their brown patterns, their speed and the females' habit of carrying their cocoons attached to their spinnerets, the spiders of the family Lycosidae are numerous in all parts of the temperate zone. But the careful collector finds that different species are found in different kinds of surroundings, and the type-genus Lycosa is sufficient to illustrate this. The two species *Lycosa pullata* and *L. amentata* are ubiquitous, save only that the latter is missing from the driest places: in fields and open land generally are *L. nigriceps,* *L. tarsalis,* and *L. prativaga*; *L. lugubris* is the inhabitant of woods: *L. proxima* of marshes: *L. arenicola* and *L. purbeckensis* live on the shingle of the beaches: *L. agricola* prefers the sandy banks of lakes and rivers: while *L. trailli* climbs the hills and mountains.

Here is obviously a far more complex problem than that of the two Zygiellas, and no solution is as yet forthcoming; it shows how well spiders are suited to such ecological questions as may be asked at every visit to a Field Centre or at every attempt to systematize one's observations.

The Lycosidae-problem leads to the complementary type of study. Instead of asking where the different members of a genus, a family or any other group are to be found, we may alternatively ask what different spiders are to be found in any one particular and definable area.

The nature of the area or station chosen for such work as this must of course depend on what may be easily accessible from the ecologist's home, and its size must be related to the number of observers who are collaborating in the project. For a solitary arachnologist the area can hardly be too small.

Probably the most obvious kind of station to choose is a pond. Ponds are numerous, pond-searchers have long since developed the technique that suits the conditions, and ponds are attractive to spiders and harvestmen. Moreover, a pond readily defines the exact region under observation.

Almost as well defined is a quarry. It is immaterial whether the quarry yields chalk or slate or granite or anything else, for it is nearly always a place with plenty of loose rock on the ground, providing good shelter for small animals, and also a place with vertical rock-faces, sunny or shaded or both. Further, many small animals find it easier to fall into a quarry than to climb out of it, so that it may become a focus or point of concentration, an ecological analogue of a human city.

Similarly, stretches of the seashore, of a hedgerow, of a river bank, of the edge of a wood, or a clearing within a wood may be chosen, and will provide suitable areas.

The traditional method is, first, by intensive collecting, to determine the species that inhabit the station. Then to revisit the area and repeat the census at regular intervals throughout the year, noting in particular the arrival of new species and the absence of others.

Monthly intervals are usually sufficient: they are not frequent

D

enough to become tedious, and they give time enough between one expedition and the next to identify the species in the bag. A year's work of this kind gives precise information about the population of the site, about the seasonal variation and therefore about the life-histories of the different species present. Some may be found as adults throughout the year, some only in the spring, others only in the autumn. Many will not appear during certain months, when they exist only as eggs.

A year's ecology in a station does not complete all that may be done nor give all the information it can yield. It is possible to supplement the collecting by distinguishing ground-level species, species of the undergrowth and species of the hedgetops and trees. It is possible, if the enthusiasm suffices, to compare species active during the day with the always surprisingly large number of species that are active at night and can be watched in the beam of a good electric torch.

A most important point is that all ecological work is of value only in so far as the species encountered have been correctly named. There are many groups of small animals where the identifications of the beginner are open to question, and need confirmation. In fact it has been said that the accumulation of specimens and their submission to experts is a practice that has been raised to the status of a new science and called ecology. This is unkind, but it holds an element of truth.

The ecologist who accumulates spiders is fortunate in this respect. Immature specimens can always be put into their correct families and often into their correct genera, and recorded as "sp. juv.", which is a Latin abbreviation for "a young one". Mature specimens are determinable by the form of their genitalia, which are all illustrated in the Ray Society's book, *British Spiders*, mentioned later. In many other countries helpful books of the same character are to be found, covering at least the commonest species. The determination of rare or new species is, however, a much more difficult task, generally to be undertaken only by specialists.

10   *Bibliography*

1. Berland, L. *Les Arachnides.* Lechevalier, Paris. 1932.
   Almost a French equivalent of *The Biology of Spiders* (13) but better illustrated, and written with a specialist's knowledge of the order.

2. Bonnet, P. *Bibliographia Araneorum.* Douladoure, Toulouse. 1945-62.
   A complete bibliography of all that had been published about spiders, from the earliest times to 1939, together with biographies of arachnologists and much other information.

3. Bristowe, W. S. *The Comity of Spiders.* Ray Society, London. Vol. 1, 1939; Vol. 2, 1942.
   The first volume gives a list of all species of British spiders known at the time of writing, and adds their distribution in all the counties. There are also accounts of the spiders found in many different ecological niches, of their food, their enemies, their dispersal, their courtship and general behaviour.

4. Bristowe, W. S. *The World of Spiders.* Collins, London. 1958.
   One of the New Naturalist series, and an attractive record of the ways of spiders and of the enjoyment that may be derived

from a lifetime given to their study. The book deals with history, systematics and biology, and its numerous illustrations are accurate and artistic above the average.

5. Bronn, H. G. *Klassen und Ordnungen des Tierreichs.* Leipsig. 1934-43.

Books 4 to 8 of the Fourth Part deal with the taxonomy of the Arachnida, their structure, development and general biology.

6. Cloudsley-Thompson, J. L. *Spiders, Scorpions, Centipedes and Mites.* Pergamon Press, Oxford. 1958.

A natural history of high zoological standard, concerned to describe the lives, habits and behaviour of a number of rather unfamiliar arthropods.

7. Gertsch, W. J. *American Spiders.* Van Nostrand, New York. 1949.

A comprehensive account of the biology of American spiders, authoritatively written and extremely well illustrated. One of the American New Naturalist series.

8. Grassé, P. P. *Traité de Zoologie.* Masson, Paris. 1949–.

The first published part of this great work was Tome VI, which devotes about a thousand pages to the Arachnida.

9. Kükenthal, W. and Krumbach, T. *Handbuch der Zoologie.* Gruyter, Berlin. 1932-38.

The second half of the third volume of this immense work on zoology is devoted to the Arachnida and comprises nearly 700 large pages, fully illustrated.

10. Locket, G. H. and Millidge, A. F. *British Spiders.* Ray Society, London. Vol. 1, 1951; Vol. 2, 1953.

This is the standard systematic work on the spiders of Britain and is likely to retain its pre-eminence for many years. It begins with a short history of arachnology in Britain, written by W. S. Bristowe, and describes all the British species, then known to be 581 in number. There are keys to the genera of every family, and accurate illustrations of the female epigyne and male palp of every species.

11. McKeown, K. C. *Australian Spiders*. Angus and Robertson, Sydney. 1951.
A successful account of the lives and habits of many of Australia's most conspicuous arachnids.

12. Roewer, C. F. *Katalog der Araneen*. Vol. 1, Bremen, 1940; Vol. 2, Brussels, 1954.
An immense catalogue of 2790 pages in all, a storehouse of information on the nomenclature of spiders.

13. Savory, T. H. *The Biology of Spiders*. Sidgwick and Jackson, London. 1928.
An attempt to bring together in one volume the essentials of the then existing knowledge of spiders. Its bibliography is a guide to the early researches which laid the foundations of arachnology, half a century and more ago.

14. Savory, T. H. *Spiders, Men and Scorpions*. Univ. of London Press, London. 1961.
A history of the growth of the science of arachnology from the earliest times.

15. Yaginuma, T. *Spiders of Japan in Colour*. Hoikusha, Osaka. 1960.
Few of us can read about spiders in the Japanese language, but this book compels mention because it is a superb production, with 320 incomparable coloured drawings, a book which the Western World has nothing to equal or to approach.

Index